Corporate Governance

Duties and Responsibilities of Boards in Company Groups

Please cite this publication as:
OECD (2020), *Duties and Responsibilities of Boards in Company Groups*, Corporate Governance, OECD Publishing, Paris, *https://doi.org/10.1787/859ec8fe-en*.

ISBN 978-92-64-75208-5 (print)
ISBN 978-92-64-40145-7 (pdf)

Corporate Governance
ISSN 2077-6527 (print)
ISSN 2077-6535 (online)

Photo credits: Cover © KrulUA/iStock/Getty Images Plus.

Corrigenda to publications may be found on line at: *www.oecd.org/about/publishing/corrigenda.htm*.

Foreword

This report presents the results of the peer review on the duties and responsibilities of boards in company groups carried out by the OECD Corporate Governance Committee. The Committee regularly undertakes such comparative reviews as part of its mandate to monitor and support implementation of the G20/OECD Principles of Corporate Governance, and to respond to emerging corporate governance challenges.

The report presents an overview of the legal/regulatory framework (including corporate governance codes) with respect to board duties and responsibilities in group companies in 45 jurisdictions, and it identifies different approaches to the common phenomena of group structures.

The report is primarily based on responses to a questionnaire sent to Committee delegates in June 2019. The report is complemented by case studies prepared by four jurisdictions: Colombia, India, Israel and Korea. These case studies and the overview chapter were discussed at the Committee's April and October 2019 meetings, and this final version of the report takes account of both of these discussions as well as subsequent written comments received from Committee delegates.

The overview chapter of this publication was written by Mike Lubrano, under the oversight of Mats Isaksson, Daniel Blume and Serdar Çelik of the OECD Directorate for Financial and Enterprise Affairs, with additional support from Kenta Fukami, Adriana De La Cruz, Tugba Mulazimoglu, Chung-a Park, Yun Tang, Katrina Baker and Anaísa Gonçalves. The country case study chapters were prepared by the respective authorities of each country: for Colombia, Jorge Castaño Gutierrez, Francisco Duque, María Ganan, Samira Gamboa, Tomas Castaneda and Angelica Osorio of the Financial Superintendency of Colombia (SFC) with additional contribution from the Superintendency of Companies; for India, Pradeep Ramakrishnan, Nila Khanolkar and Ishita Sharma under the supervision of Gurumoorthy Mahalingam of the Securities and Exchange Board of India (SEBI); for Israel, Ronnie Talmore of the Ministry of Justice and Offir Eyal of the Israel Securities Authority (ISA); and for Korea, Moonok Bang of the Korea Corporate Governance Service (KCGS) with oversight from Dr. Myeong Hyeon Cho of the Korea University Business School and Korea Corporate Governance Service (KCGS) and Haemi Yi of the Commercial Legal Affairs Division of the Ministry of Justice. Special thanks are extended to the Committee delegates from all 45 participating jurisdictions who provided responses to the questionnaire and useful comments throughout the development of this report.

Table of contents

FIGURES

TABLES

Executive summary

Corporate ownership through company groups is a common and sometimes the preponderant pattern of shareholding in an important number of markets. Data on share ownership by corporations and affiliated individuals indicates that a significant portion of publicly-listed companies in many of the markets surveyed for this report are members of a company group.

Previous OECD reports identified important advantages and benefits to carrying out entrepreneurial activity through affiliated but legally separate companies, including scale economies, efficiencies in resource allocation, reduced dependence on external finance, fewer informational asymmetries, lower transaction costs and less reliance on contract enforcement. Protection of intellectual property rights and facilitation of cross-border activity are additional common rationales. These advantages and benefits, among others, continue to make company groups important contributors to economic development and employment generation in many markets.

From a corporate governance policy perspective, company groups present the same agency problems that face stand-alone companies with defined control. Notably, parent companies may attempt to appropriate undue private benefits of control. Since cooperation in pursuit of synergies is a key rationale for company groups, groups typically engage in frequent related-party transactions. The more complex the structure of a group, the greater the opportunity for such transactions to be carried out in a less transparent fashion, which may benefit some group companies at the expense of others. Like other majority shareholders, parent companies in groups may engage in transactions that do not benefit all shareholders equally, such as intra-group mergers and sales of control to third parties effected on questionable terms. Allocation of business opportunities is another area that can present conflicts of interest for boards, individual directors and managers of group companies.

Groups also present non-agency-related issues. Domination of an economy by groups, may slow the development of broader, deeper and more efficient national capital markets. The organisation of industry into networks of related companies may also reduce competition in product and service markets.

The challenge of regulation of company groups is to secure the benefits that company groups can confer while managing the potential risks of abuse and inequitable treatment of shareholders and other stakeholders. It is important in this process to view properly-crafted group company law and regulation as a means to foster legal certainty to enable the achievement of greater synergies and efficiencies. Clarity around the rules and expectations for how company groups should operate allows entrepreneurs, directors and employees to focus more on value creation and less on protecting against litigation or regulatory intervention.

Approaches to the challenges of company group structures for directors and boards

The threshold question for a discussion of the duties and responsibilities of boards in company groups is— To whom do directors of group companies owe their fiduciary duties? The responses to the survey questionnaire on this question fell into three general categories: (1) jurisdictions that follow the classic fiduciary approach that duties always and exclusively relate to the company (and its shareholders) on whose board the director sits; (2) jurisdictions with special frameworks that recognise exceptions to the classic fiduciary approach for certain group companies and explicitly regulate such exceptions; and (3) jurisdictions where there have been efforts to somehow reconcile the classic approach to the group context without explicitly creating a separate group company regime modifying directors' duties and/or to whom they are owed.

More than three-fourths of jurisdictions surveyed fall into the first category. Ten responding jurisdictions may be split between the remaining two categories, reporting that their legal/regulatory frameworks provide some form of separate regime for the duties and responsibilities of directors and boards of group companies. Most of these share some elements of Germany's *Konzernrecht* ("company groups law") concept. Importantly, practically all questionnaire responses evidenced legal/regulatory provisions and self-regulatory efforts to at least partially address the risks of mistreatment of shareholders and other stakeholders that group structures present. These provisions can generally be grouped into the following categories:

a. guidance on when and how directors may take into account group interests
b. clarity of procedures for managing conflicts of interest
c. processes for compensating losses incurred by a group company for the benefit of the group
d. transparency around group purposes and allocation of business opportunities
e. allocation of responsibility for company policy and oversight between parent and subsidiary boards (group governance)[1]

Observations and policy issues

This report is a stocktaking of current issues, practices and policy approaches with respect to the duties and responsibilities of boards in company groups. It does not evaluate the relative advantages and disadvantages of the legal/regulatory and self-regulatory approaches reported by respondents. The survey results do, however, shed light on aspects of the framework for board duties and responsibilities in company groups that have been the subject of attention in a number of jurisdictions, or where the framework does not address or remains uncertain around policy issues of relevance to company groups:

- Mandatory public disclosure of items of importance in group situations is still not required by all jurisdictions. Companies in a number of reporting jurisdictions are not required to publicly disclose major shareholders, ultimate beneficial ownership, corporate group structures, special voting rights, shareholder agreements, cross shareholdings and shareholdings of directors.
- Black letter law in most jurisdictions does not seem to directly address a parent company's and its board's usually privileged access to information from a subsidiary.
- Soft law (codes and self-regulatory efforts) may help clarify expectations and best practices, but risks legal challenge if the legal/regulatory framework is not consistent.
- There appears to be greater confidence in the efficacy of legal/regulatory frameworks around board duties to review related-party transactions than there is with respect to allocation of business/corporate opportunities among group companies.
- Explicit requirements for parent company board oversight of key risks, including compliance and supply chain risks, diverge considerably across jurisdictions.
- While judicial "piercing of the corporate veil" is rare in all jurisdictions, parent company accountability for environmental impacts and human rights in some jurisdictions has increased.

1 Overview of the legal/regulatory framework with respect to the duties and responsibilities of boards in company groups

This chapter provides an overview of the legal/regulatory framework (including corporate governance codes) with respect to board duties and responsibilities in group companies. It identifies different approaches to the common phenomena of group structures in 45 jurisdictions, including many of the world's largest economies in OECD, G20 and Financial Stability Board members. The introduction provides background on the global landscape of company groups, and summarises the economic benefits and rationale for their existence, as well as the principle challenges these economic combinations present for policy-makers. Part I provides a typology of approaches to the challenges presented by company group structures with respect to the duties and responsibilities of boards of directors. Part II elaborates on salient differences and commonalities across jurisdictions.

Background

The Financial Stability Board (FSB) conducted a peer review on the implementation of the G20/OECD Principles of Corporate Governance for publicly listed regulated financial institutions. The Chair of the FSB's review team presented the preliminary results of the review to the Corporate Governance Committee in November 2016. The final recommendations from the FSB review were published in April 2017 and included a proposal to the OECD for a follow-up review on the practices with respect to the effectiveness of rules regarding the duties, responsibilities and composition of boards within group structures.

Against this background, the Committee agreed, at its meeting in April 2018, that a background report on the *Duties and Responsibilities of Boards in Company Group Structures* should be developed for an exploratory roundtable discussion in the October 2018 meeting. The background report, developed by Professor, Dr. jur. Karsten Engsig Sørensen, was submitted to the Committee for discussion at the October 2018 roundtable meeting. A scoping paper setting out the framework for a review of the duties of boards in company groups together with a proposed roadmap and options for conducting the work was also submitted to the Committee for discussion at that meeting. Finally, the report *Corporate Governance of Company Groups in Latin America*, which was developed by the *Latin American Corporate Governance Roundtable's Task Force on Company Groups* was also submitted to the Committee as background for the roundtable discussion. These reports provide an overview of the different benefits of and rationales for the establishment of company groups and some of the most relevant issues with respect to corporate governance and board duties that announce themselves in group structures.

At its meeting in October 2018, the Committee agreed to conduct a peer review on the *Duties and Responsibilities of Boards in Company Group Structures* and to collect information from all jurisdictions via a questionnaire sent to delegates. The draft questionnaire was submitted to the Committee for discussion and feedback at its April 2019 meeting before being finalised and sent to delegates in June 2019. In all, 45 jurisdictions responded to the questionnaire (See Annex A. " Questionnaire" for the full questionnaire).

Structure and content of the questionnaire; responses; structure of this report

The principal elements of legal/regulatory frameworks with respect to the duties and responsibilities of boards in company group structures addressed in the questionnaire included:

a. definition
b. disclosure and transparency
c. group structures
d. composition, structure and function of group company boards
e. duties and responsibilities of group company directors
f. powers of parent companies over subsidiaries
g. coordinated activities and intra-group transactions
h. responsibility for parent companies and other group members for the acts of a group member

The Committee received responses from 45 jurisdictions. The Introduction to this chapter provides background on the global landscape of company groups. It summarises the economic benefits of and rationale for their existence and describes the principle challenges these economic combinations present for policy makers. Part I follows with a typology of approaches to the challenges presented by company group structures with respect to the duties and responsibilities of boards and directors, drawing from the questionnaire responses, subsequent communications with several respondents, the case studies prepared by Colombia, India, Israel and Korea, earlier work of the Committee and other relevant work on this topic.

Part II elaborates on salient differences and commonalities across jurisdictions apparent from the responses in the following areas:

a. definition of company groups and their members
b. limitations on permissible group structures
c. transparency of group structures and operations
d. composition, structure and functioning of boards and committees
e. parent company board responsibility for oversight and governance of the group
f. information flows within the company group
g. misuse of subsidiaries to avoid compliance with legal obligations of listed companies
h. liability of parent companies for acts or omissions of subsidiaries

Introduction

Prevalence of company groups

The legal/regulatory framework with respect to the duties and responsibilities of boards in company group structures is important for three principal reasons: (1) concentrated ownership, very often taking the form of company groups, is a common and sometimes the preponderant pattern of shareholding in an important number of markets; (2) well-managed company groups can contribute importantly to economic development and employment through achievement of economies of scale, synergies and other efficiencies; but (3) company group structures present the potential for inequitable treatment of shareholders and other stakeholders and other negative consequences for the efficiency and development of capital markets and economies more broadly.

The Committee's regional roundtables in Asia, Middle East and North Africa and Latin America have all identified the important presence of company groups and holding companies in the corporate sectors of the respective regions. An OECD review of the distribution of ownership of publicly listed companies globally indicates a strong presence of company groups not only in emerging economies but also in many European countries. To provide a global overview, Table 1.1, below, shows the distribution of publicly listed companies among different categories of owners, including private corporations and holding companies.

Table 1.1 reveals that private corporations and holding companies is the largest category of owners in nine of the jurisdictions surveyed. In several Asian economies, including India, Indonesia and Singapore, and some other emerging markets such as Argentina, Brazil, Chile and Turkey, private corporations and holding companies hold more than 30% of the total equity capital in publicly listed companies. In other Asian economies, including Korea and Malaysia, and several European markets, including Austria, France, Greece and Poland, private corporations on average hold between 18 to 24% of the capital. The significant levels of ownership by private corporations and holding companies in publicly listed companies is probably one of the reasons for an increased interest in the characteristics of company groups and the responsibilities of board and directors in such groups.

Table 1.1 Ownership by different categories of owners in publicly listed companies in selected jurisdictions, as a percentage of total capital, as of end 2017

	Private corporations	Public sector	Strategic individuals	Institutional investors	Other free-float
Chile	**55%**	1%	14%	12%	18%
Turkey	**40%**	14%	10%	17%	18%
India	**37%**	17%	8%	20%	19%
Indonesia	**36%**	20%	12%	11%	21%
Brazil	**34%**	13%	8%	25%	20%
Argentina	**32%**	18%	13%	19%	18%
Singapore	**30%**	12%	11%	12%	34%
Israel	**25%**	1%	16%	25%	33%
Korea	**24%**	12%	10%	20%	34%
Austria	**24%**	16%	6%	26%	27%
Poland	**23%**	17%	8%	33%	19%
Malaysia	**22%**	40%	7%	12%	19%
Russia	**20%**	32%	14%	12%	21%
Mexico	**20%**	1%	34%	20%	25%
South Africa	**19%**	15%	5%	34%	27%
Greece	**19%**	13%	13%	19%	36%
Japan	**18%**	11%	3%	37%	31%
France	**18%**	7%	11%	28%	36%
Netherlands	**18%**	4%	6%	46%	27%
Germany	**15%**	6%	7%	34%	39%
Sweden	**14%**	7%	11%	38%	31%
Hong Kong, China	**13%**	38%	10%	12%	27%
China	**11%**	38%	13%	9%	28%
Italy	**10%**	12%	15%	29%	34%
Norway	**8%**	34%	7%	29%	21%
Canada	**8%**	4%	2%	47%	39%
United Kingdom	**7%**	7%	2%	63%	22%
Finland	**5%**	14%	9%	35%	37%
United States	**2%**	3%	4%	72%	19%

Notes: The market capitalisation coverage ratio for each market is 85% or greater (except for Israel and Finland where it is 82%). "Other free-float" refers to the shares in the hands of investors that are not required to disclose their holdings. It includes the direct holdings of retail investors who are not required to disclose their ownership and institutional investors that do not exceed the required thresholds for public disclosure of their holdings.

Source: De La Cruz, A., A. Medina and Y. Tang (2019), "Owners of the World's Listed Companies", OECD Capital Market Series, Paris.

In addition to the data in Table 1.1, there are two other aspects of ownership that warrant particular attention with respect to the importance of corporate groups. The first is the presence of strategic individual investors, representing controlling or blockholder individuals or families who in many cases may be linked to the corporate groups. For example, while corporations and holding companies hold on average 20% of the capital in listed Mexican companies, another 34% is owned by strategic individuals and families. The second is public sector ownership, which also plays an important role in several markets, including Hong Kong, China); Malaysia Norway; People's Republic of China (hereafter 'China') and Russia, with an average ownership ratio above 30% of the outstanding capital. Many jurisdictions have also established holding companies for substantial portfolios of state-owned enterprises, including listed companies.

To broaden the perspective, Figure 1.1 focuses on companies where one private corporation or a holding company is the largest shareholder of a listed company. It shows both the share of companies where a corporation is the largest holder and the average size of its holding. The figure covers almost 8 000 large listed companies from 29 jurisdictions, of which 2 510 (33%) have another corporation as their largest shareholder. For example, 43% of companies in France have another corporation as the largest shareholder, holding on average 50% of the capital. Corporate ownership is quite strong also in Argentina, Chile, India, Indonesia, Israel, Korea, Malaysia and Turkey, where more than half of the companies have a corporation as the largest shareholder. These data seem to confirm the presence of private corporations and holding companies as an important category of owners in listed companies and in many cases also the presence of group structures that include one or several listed companies.

Figure 1.1. Corporations as the largest shareholders

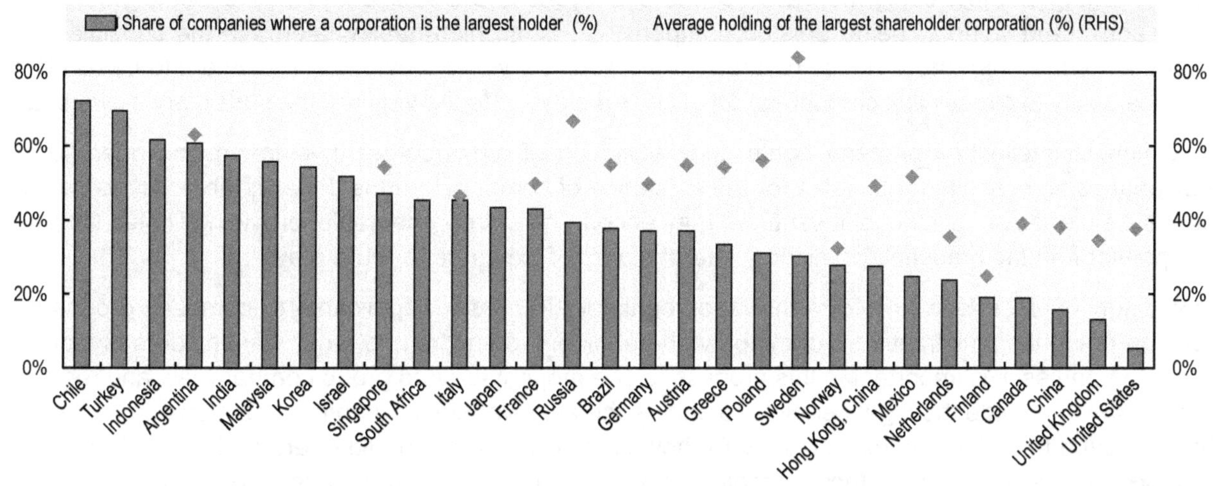

Source: De La Cruz, A., A. Medina and Y. Tang (2019), "Owners of the World's Listed Companies", OECD Capital Market Series, Paris.

It is important to note that while concentration of ownership of capital is a principal indicator of control at the company level, there are several arrangements available in corporate governance frameworks that allow control without holding a majority of the company's actual equity capital. These include multiple class share structures, shareholder agreements, special voting rules, cross-shareholdings and pyramid structures.[2] And, of course, in companies with more dispersed shareholding and/or low turnout at shareholder meetings, a single shareholder may still have significant influence and sometimes effectively control the shareholder meeting with less than a majority of the company's voting shares.

Advantages and benefits of company groups

Consistent with Principle II.F ("Related-party transactions should be approved and conducted in a manner that ensures proper management of conflict of interest and protects the interest of the company and its shareholders"), the Committee has directed considerable attention to studying and confronting the issues of related-party transactions, both within and outside the context of company groups. The OECD-Asian Roundtable on Corporate Governance's *Guide on Fighting Abusive Related Party Transactions in Asia* was released in September 2009 and *Related Party Transactions and Minority Shareholder Rights*, presenting the results of the third thematic peer review based on the *OECD Principles of Corporate Governance*, was published in 2012.

While both documents focused on efforts in many jurisdictions to minimise the negative potential of self-dealing, the fact that virtually no jurisdiction bans all related-party transactions outright reflects, among other things, a broad recognition of the important benefits of intra-group coordination and transactions—"consensus accepts that related party transactions can be economically beneficial, especially in company groups where there are other developmental arguments that they substitute for under-developed markets and institutions."[3]

Corporate Governance of Company Groups in Latin America, published by OECD in 2015, included a subchapter on the benefits of and economic rationale for corporate groups. Positive contributions of properly-managed company groups cited in that study include efficiencies in resource allocation, reduced need for external finance (internalised capital markets), fewer informational asymmetries, lower transaction costs and less reliance on (often unreliable) contract enforcement mechanisms.

More recently, the results of a 2018 survey conducted by Japan's Ministry of Economy, Trade and Industry reported the following top four benefits/rationales cited by parent companies for owning a listed subsidiary: (1) maintaining and improving motivation of the employees of the subsidiary; (2) maintaining the higher-status and brand value of being a listed company; (3) hiring high-quality talents in the subsidiary; and (4) ensuring trust with the business partners of the subsidiary.[4] An obvious complement to items (1) and (3) is the ability to directly link compensation of key employees to the value of the subsidiary's own shares.

Protection of intellectual property rights and facilitation of cross-border investment and operation are additional commonly cited rationales for the existence of company groups. Finally, the ability to establish listed subsidiaries or unlisted joint ventures may encourage entrepreneurship, providing limited liability for the sponsor and the prospect for minority shareholders of exposure to "pure plays".

Accordingly, while efforts to reform the legal/regulatory framework applicable to company groups often focus on preventing mistreatment of minority shareholders, creditors and other stakeholders of individual group companies, it is important in this process to see properly-crafted group company law and regulation as a means to provide the legal certainty to enable the achievement of greater synergies and efficiencies. Clarity around the rules and expectations for how company groups should operate allows entrepreneurs, directors and employees to focus greater effort on value creation and less on protecting against unexpected litigation or regulatory intervention. Formation of company groups also can foster greater integration of markets across borders, which has motivated much of the European Union's attention to the topic. All these can contribute positively to economic growth and employment.

Governance challenges presented by company groups

The agency problem has historically dominated the corporate governance debate. And policy makers, practitioners and academics have focused most of their discussions around the governance of firms on an individual basis. So it should not surprise that when the topic shifts to issues around company groups, the agency focus remains.

There are, of course, good reasons for this. Company groups present all the potential agency problems that face stand-alone companies with defined control. Parent companies, like other majority or controlling shareholders, may attempt to appropriate undue private benefits of control at the expense of other shareholders and stakeholders. Since cooperation in pursuit of synergies is a key rationale for the existence of company groups, companies in such groups typically engage in frequent related-party transactions. Cash pooling is common in company groups, as are other intra-group arrangements, including joint borrowing, cross-guarantees, common branding, use of intellectual property (trademarks, patents and copyrights) and shared management services.[5] In vertically-integrated groups, frequent business transactions between parent and subsidiary are an integral part of the business model. The more complex the structure of a company group, the greater the opportunity for such transactions and arrangements to be carried out in a less transparent fashion, which may benefit some group companies at the expense of others. Like other majority shareholders, parent companies in groups may engage in transactions that do not benefit all shareholders equally, such as intra-group mergers and sales of control to third parties effected on questionable terms.

Allocation of business opportunities is an area where company groups present particular agency challenges. Companies in groups often engage in overlapping activities. A business opportunity presented to or developed by the group can frequently represent a potentially profitable activity that more than one of its member companies might be positioned to pursue. Deciding which company in the group takes up a new business idea can present conflicts of interest for boards, individual directors and managers of group companies.

Groups also present non-agency-related issues, some with potentially important macro-economic impacts. Domination of an economy by company groups, especially those that are diversified across industries and that internalise financing, may ultimately slow the development of broader, deeper and more efficient national capital markets. The organisation of industry into networks of related companies can reduce competition in product and service markets. This anti-competitive effect can be especially problematic in smaller economies. Indeed, one of the principle objectives of the reforms discussed in the Israel case study was an effort to promote greater competition.

The prominence of company groups has raised concerns in some jurisdictions that concentration of economic power in fewer hands can bring with it adverse effects. Instances of regulatory capture, rent-seeking and corruption of the political system have all been cited as associated with company groups. In the end, the challenge of regulation of company groups is to secure the recognised micro- and macroeconomic benefits that company groups can confer while managing the potential risk of abuse and inequitable treatment of shareholders and other stakeholders.

Part I. A typology of approaches to the challenges of company group structures

The *G20/OECD Principles of Corporate Governance* recognise that "[a] particular issue arises in some jurisdictions where groups of companies are prevalent and where the duty of loyalty of a board member might be ambiguous and even interpreted as to the group."[6] It follows that the threshold question for a discussion of the duties and responsibilities of boards in company group structures is—To whom do directors of group companies owe their fiduciary duties of care and loyalty? The responses to the questionnaire on this key issue can be usefully divided into three categories: (1) jurisdictions that reported that they follow the classic fiduciary approach (that duties always and exclusively relate to the company (and its shareholders) on whose board the director sits); (2) jurisdictions with special frameworks that recognise exceptions to the classic fiduciary approach for certain group companies and explicitly regulate such exceptions; and (3) jurisdictions where there have been efforts to somehow reconcile the classic approach to the group context without explicitly creating a separate group company regime modifying directors' duties and/or to whom they are owed.

Classic fiduciary duties approach

More than three-fourths (35) of jurisdictions reported that the duties and responsibilities of directors and boards in group companies are generally identical to those in companies that are not part of a group, and that each director's duties of loyalty and care relate exclusively to the company on whose board the director sits. This approach is reflected in the annotation to Principle VI.A: "It is also a key principle for board members who are working within the structure of a group of companies: even though a company might be controlled by another enterprise, the duty of loyalty for a board member relates to the company and all its shareholders and not to the controlling company of the group."

It is well-established in common law jurisdictions, including respondents Hong Kong, China; Ireland; Israel; New Zealand; United Kingdom and the United States, that the fiduciary duties of directors and boards relate solely to the company itself and not to its parent or the larger group. This is complemented in the United States (Delaware corporate law) by fiduciary duties imposed on controlling shareholders to act in the best interests of the company and in the United Kingdom, where listing rules provide special governance requirements for premium-listed companies with a controlling shareholder. Ireland's response to the questionnaire elaborates a bit on what can be described as this traditional approach: "Directors of a subsidiary are expected to run the subsidiary as an autonomous entity and directors must act in the interests of the company. The common law position would suggest that if they are nominated to the board of the subsidiary by the parent company, they may take into account the interests of the parent if there is no conflict of interest between the two companies. In the event of a conflict, however, they must, without exception, act in the interests of the company."

Restatement of the classic approach was by no means limited to the responses from common law jurisdictions. For example, France, birthplace of the Rozenblum doctrine discussed below (See Box 1.2), stated that the French legal/regulatory framework does not contain any exceptions to a director's fiduciary duties of loyalty and care to the company on whose board such director serves when the company is part of a group. China echoed the view of most other non-common law jurisdictions subscribing to the classic fiduciary duties approach, that subsidiary companies are autonomous entities and not to be regarded as subordinate to the interests of their parent companies or the group of companies with which they are associated.

Special frameworks for companies in groups

Ten responding jurisdictions reported that their legal/regulatory frameworks, recognising the special characteristics of certain company groups, provide some form of separate regime for the duties and responsibilities of directors and boards of group companies. Most of these share at least some of the elements of the *Konzernrecht* ("law on company groups") concept, first introduced into German company law in 1965 (See Box 1.1).

Box 1.1 *Konzernrecht*—The German model of company group governance

Several jurisdictions within and outside the European Union have followed or have been influenced by Germany's autonomous body of company group law (*Konzernrecht*—generally translated as "law on company groups"). This model contemplates two types of company groups: *de facto* and contractual. *De facto* groups exist when one company owns shares or voting rights in another company that grants it effective control. In such cases the negative impact of any influence of the former (parent) over the latter (subsidiary) must be disclosed, audited and compensated. Under the German law, compensation must be time-bound. In general, compensation should be effected in the same fiscal year in which the subsidiary's losses are realised.

Shareholders of a company whose board declares that the negative impact caused by the parent was not sufficiently compensated can request a special investigation of the circumstances. The parent and its directors can be held liable to the subsidiary for uncompensated losses. They may also be held liable to the shareholders of the subsidiary for additional damages arising from impairment of the share price. The directors and members of the supervisory board of the subsidiary can also be held liable to the company's shareholders if they did not act with due care or concealed the extent of the negative impact on the company caused by the parent.

Celebration of a Control Agreement between the parent company and its subsidiary creates a contractual group. The Control Agreement must be approved by the shareholders of both companies and must bind the parent company to compensate the subsidiary for losses on an annual basis (thereby preserving the latter's capital for the protection of creditors and potentially other stakeholders). Control Agreements typically also provide for transfer of profits to the parent, fixed dividends and put (exit) rights for shareholders of the subsidiary.

In both cases, directors and boards of subsidiaries are protected from liability for violation of the duty of loyalty so long as they can show they exercised due care to ensure that adequate compensation was determined and paid in the case of *de facto* groups and that the terms of the Control Agreement were respected in the case of contractual groups.

Among the respondents to the questionnaire, Latvia, Portugal and Slovenia (with Austria, mostly through case law) have incorporated much of the German model into their national company law regimes. Others, including Brazil, Czech Republic and Poland, have incorporated certain elements of the contractual group concept.

Among the legislation cited in the responses, Latvia's Group of Companies Law and Slovenia's Companies Act appear to draw most heavily on the German model for inspiration.[7] Each law posits dominant and dependent entities under the unified management of the dominant entity. Such groups (or "concerns") benefit from explicit recognition that the dependent entities may be managed for the benefit of the controller and specify procedures for determining the compensation due the dependent entity for its sacrifices. For the protection of creditors and other stakeholders, the legislation also typically imposes certain liabilities on the parent company and sets limits on what the dominant entity can cause the dependent entity to do. To the extent that they operate within these frameworks, directors in group companies are effectively excused from their duty of loyalty to the specific group company on whose board they serve. Such directors are not, however, relieved of their duty of care. For example, directors of subsidiary companies can be held responsible for failure to adequately oversee compliance with the specified procedures for determining the compensation due the company.

Similarly, the Portuguese Companies Code provides that a parent company forms a group together with those companies it manages in accordance with a subordination agreement, along with all its wholly-owned subsidiaries. "Under article 503 of the [Companies Code], the parent company has the right to issue binding instructions to a subsidiary's board. Such instructions may be disadvantageous to the subsidiary if they serve the parent company's interests or other group company's interests. Therefore ... the subsidiary's board members shall not be liable for any acts or omissions committed when executing the instructions received."[8] Portugal's response noted that the requirements for compensation provided in its legislation are on balance more flexible and less time-bound than in German law and practice.[9]

Other jurisdictions highlighted in their responses the possibility of contractual arrangements within the legal/regulatory framework applicable to company groups. Poland's Code of Commercial Companies provides for an agreement between a parent and a subsidiary allowing the parent company to manage the subsidiary and/or to transfer profit from the subsidiary. Such agreements should also determine the scope of liability of the parent company for damages for breach of the agreement and the scope of responsibility of the parent for liabilities of the subsidiary to creditors. The legality of these sorts of contractual arrangements is also supported by the Polish Civil Code's general provisions permitting freedom of contract between private parties.

New Zealand and the Netherlands both reported legislation providing an option for amending the duties and responsibilities of directors and boards in group situations. New Zealand's Companies Act specifically provides that the charter of a subsidiary may alter the duties of its directors to enable them to "act in a way which they believe is in the best interests of that company's holding company, even though it may not be in the best interests of the [subsidiary]. Such a charter provision must be approved by agreement of the shareholders, excluding the holding company. (There is no corresponding ability to modify duty of care.)" However, in the case of listed companies, only independent directors may vote to take such action, and consent of the minority shareholders is required. So as a practical matter, listed companies very rarely, if ever, avail themselves of this exception to the directors' duty of loyalty. The Civil Code of the Netherlands provides that a company's articles of association may provide that its directors must act in accordance with instructions from its (controlling) shareholders "in regards general guidelines on areas set in the articles of association". However, the Dutch Civil Code also provides that such directors should ignore such instructions if to follow them would be "contrary to the interests of the company and the enterprises connected with it".

Squaring the circle? Rozenblum, other balancing approaches and self-regulation

The challenge for any legal framework's treatment of directors' duties in company groups, especially in those where the classic fiduciary duties approach is regarded as "black letter law", is squaring itself with the legitimate purposes for which company groups exist and the actual behaviour of directors and boards. Companies in groups observably act differently from their stand-alone company peers, with the strong implication that their boards work in importantly different ways. The challenge for both boards and policy makers is working through the practical difficulties, both informational and analytical, of identifying and measuring how the interests of the group and its member overlap and diverge, and promoting outcomes that are equitable and economically efficient.

While it was not mentioned in the responses to the questionnaire, the Rozenblum doctrine has proven a durable, albeit only partial, solution in those European countries that have adopted it. Rozenblum softens the general classic approach by allowing some room for directors, in the exercise of their fiduciary duties to the companies they serve, to balance the current cost of supporting other group companies with the perhaps longer-term potential benefits of group membership (as distinguished from acting at the explicit instruction of other group companies). Case law and actual practices clearly differ among jurisdictions when it comes to assessment of the possibility of future benefits deriving from group membership as adequate compensation for a subsidiary's sacrifice.

Box 1.2. The Rozenblum Doctrine

The Rozenblum doctrine originated from a 1985 case in the French Cour de Cassation, *Rozenblum et Allouche.* Although the case concerned a criminal prosecution for abuse of assets, the reasoning of the court is applied in civil claims in other jurisdictions for violation of the duty of loyalty of subsidiary company directors who take into account the interests of the parent company in making decisions.[10] Application of the doctrine protects the directors from liability for violation of the duty of loyalty where: (i) the businesses of the companies are carried out within a coherent group policy; (ii) the directors believe their actions will advance the interests of the group; (iii) the compensation is not grossly inadequate; and (iv) the actions will not bring about the effective insolvency of the subsidiary.

It should be kept in mind that the Rozenblum doctrine has important limits. First, it does not address and has not been applied in cases where the parent actually formally instructs the subsidiary to take or refrain from some action. Second, it does not absolve directors from fulfilling their duty of care. Finally, while the requirement that compensation not be grossly inadequate is notably looser than the compensation requirement under the German *Konzernrecht* regime, there has to be some sort of defensible, if general and not-time-bound, *quid pro quo*.

The Rozenblum doctrine has been influential in case law in several responding jurisdictions, including Belgium, Estonia, Netherlands and Spain.

To a greater or lesser extent, the questionnaire responses of practically all jurisdictions following the classic fiduciary duties approach (and also those that have absorbed some of the German model) evidence provisions of the legal/regulatory framework that in effect at least partially address the risks of mistreatment of shareholders and other stakeholders that group structures present. These provisions can be loosely grouped into the following categories:

a. articulation of under what circumstances, and to what extent, directors may take into account group interests (balance the costs with the benefits of group membership) without compromising their duty of loyalty to the company they serve
b. clarity of procedures for identifying and managing inherent conflicts of interest that commonly arise in company groups
c. reasonable processes for determining and compensating losses incurred by a group company for the benefit of the group
d. transparency around group purposes and encouragement of contractual and quasi-contractual arrangements that reduce conflicts of interest and shape expectations around allocation of business opportunities
e. realistic and transparent allocation of responsibility for company policy and oversight between parent and subsidiary boards (group governance)

Box 1.3. Italy—Statutory Rozenblum

Although Italian company law does not provide a definition of company group, the Italian Civil Code sets out rules for subsidiaries that are "directed and coordinated" by their parent company. To protect minority shareholders (and creditors) of a "directed and coordinated" subsidiary when such entity is not operated consistently with "principles of correct company and business management", the Italian Civil Code allows shareholders and creditors to sue the parent company for damages suffered. However, this right is tempered by Italian case law acknowledging an overall economic "group concept", with courts permitting parent companies to assert an affirmative defence that any damages suffered by the subsidiary were offset by other transactions or the totality of benefits resulting from the direction and coordination of the parent company.

This framework also allows listed subsidiaries to pursue the interests of all the companies involved in this sort of group relationship, and permits such overall (group) interests to be taken into account by the subsidiary's directors, subject to certain disclosure and procedural requirements. Accordingly, Italian securities law provides for additional requirements to be met for the listing of a subsidiary subject to direction and coordination by its parent company.

Actions taken in pursuit of the benefit of the companies under the direction and coordination of the parent are subject to the following transparency requirements:

a. detailed disclosure of the justification for the transactions entered into at the behest of the parent
b. annual report disclosure of the company's relationships with other group companies and illustration of their impact on the company's management and results
c. disclosure (in any corporate document issued by the subsidiary) that it was subject to the direction and coordination by the parent company

In the case of listed subsidiaries, additional requirements have implications for board structure and composition at the subsidiary level. A company that wishes to take advantage of this framework must declare that it is subject to direction and coordination by another entity at the time it applies for listing, and in its annual financial statements and the annual Corporate Governance Report submitted to shareholders. Additionally, Italian securities regulations require a listed subsidiary that is subject to direction and coordination by its parent company to have a risk and control committee (which oversees the audit process and internal control system) made up entirely of independent directors. Other voluntary committees of the board of the subsidiary must also be made up entirely of independent directors. If the parent company is also listed, a majority of the board of the subsidiary must be independent.

Not all Italian listed companies with a dominant shareholder come under this regime. According to the Italian securities regulator's 2018 Report on the Corporate Governance of Italian Listed Companies, of the 120 listed companies that have a majority shareholder and the 57 whose largest shareholder can exercise predominant voting rights ("weakly controlled" companies), 39 were subject to direction and coordination by another entity. Those Italian listed companies with a dominant shareholder that do not consider themselves subject to direction and control by another entity must declare the grounds for their determination in their annual management report (Italy's securities regulations provide for a transitional regime for a company that become subject to direction and control by another entity subsequent to its listing).

Self-regulation: Group protocols and group governance guidelines

The challenges for directors and the potential for conflicts among shareholders are intensified when the activities of individual companies in a group overlap, or have the potential to overlap. As noted earlier in this report, potentially profitable business opportunities may arise that the shareholders of more than one group company may reasonably expect their company is positioned and entitled to exploit. Minority shareholders of companies acquired by a group not infrequently complain that the acquisition was accomplished precisely so the parent could appropriate the subsidiary's future business opportunities. This is one rationale for equitable tender offer rules that ensure that the control premium is shared with minority shareholders.

The Spanish national code of corporate governance attempts to reduce the potential for disputes over misappropriation of business opportunities by promoting greater transparency about the expected future activities of companies within a group. Spain's code recommends that to safeguard the interests of the stakeholders in all group companies, the group should draw up and publish a protocol that: (1) clearly demarcates the areas of activity of each company in the group; and (2) creates a framework of rules to prevent possible conflicts. Making expectations of the division of business opportunities among group companies explicit can provide directors and managers greater confidence to go about their value-creating activities without undue concern that their allocation of risks and rewards will be later second-guessed.

Colombia was one of only three respondents to the survey whose national code of corporate governance includes a definition of a company group.[11] Principal among the changes included in the code's most recent amendments in 2014 was the inclusion of recommendations aimed at reducing the potential for conflicts among stakeholders of different group companies. While affirming the legal autonomy of each corporate entity, Colombia's code recognises the potential conflicts implicit in such groups and states that the functions of the board of the *parent* company should be carried out through *policies implemented with respect for the balance between the interests of the group and its members.* This balancing approach is complemented by a set of special recommendations for group companies regarding organisational structure, audit and controls, and disclosure.

"Group governance" initiatives in India and Japan appear to be in a similar vein. India's questionnaire response noted that under the SEBI (Listing Obligations and Disclosure Requirements) Regulations, 2015, listed parent companies with a large number of unlisted subsidiaries may monitor the group's governance through a dedicated group governance unit or a governance committee of the parent's board. Such monitoring is envisioned to be around compliance with the form and goals of an explicit group governance policy approved by the listed company's board. The *2nd-Term Corporate Governance Study Group* of Japan's Ministry of Economy, Trade and Industry (METI) published its *Group Guidelines* in June 2019. The Guidelines reflect the results of interviews and surveys conducted by METI with company groups in Japan and elsewhere. They encourage companies in groups to articulate how the group structure "optimize[s] the business portfolio in order to improve value for the entire corporate group". Among its practical recommendations to ensure fair treatment of minority shareholders of group companies is to increase the percentage of independent directors on the boards of listed subsidiaries and to tighten the definition of an independent director on subsidiary boards so as to exclude anyone associated with the parent company in the previous ten years.[12]

The self-regulatory efforts just described are undoubtedly promising. However, some may be exposed to challenge as incompatible with the current legal framework applicable to boards, directors and shareholder rights in jurisdictions that otherwise follow the classic fiduciary duties approach. Colombia's chapter in *Corporate Governance of Company Groups in Latin America* noted that in the absence of any specific reference to the duties of directors of parents or subsidiaries in the country's Commercial Code, there is disagreement within the Colombian legal community about whether following the recommendations of the national code of corporate governance with respect to group companies provides directors effective legal protection. This points to the need for jurisdictions considering provisions applicable to company groups in national codes or other voluntary best practice guidance to take into account the compatibility of such provisions with the existing legal framework.

Part II. Differences and commonalities in legal/regulatory treatment of company group issues revealed by the questionnaire responses

Definition of company groups and their members

A definition of a company group can be explicitly provided in law or regulation, or the concept may be defined implicitly, by separately identifying the typical elements of a group, such as parent, subsidiary, affiliate or associate company. Five jurisdictions reported that an explicit, specific definition of a "company group" is absent from their company law/regulation, securities law/regulation, listing rules, national corporate governance code or other laws. However, taking into account the comments provided by the respondents from such jurisdictions, it is fair to say that for practical effects, some form of explicit or implicit company group definition (and in many cases more than one), is provided under the current legal/regulatory regime of all reporting jurisdictions.

Table 1.2 sets out where in the legal/regulatory frameworks of the responding jurisdiction an explicit or implicit definition of company group is laid out. A solid majority of respondents (30) reported company legislation/regulations that includes criteria for when a set of companies are regarded as constituting a group. Securities laws/regulation of an important number of respondents (21) also provided a specific definition. The listing rules of only nine jurisdictions included specific reference to company groups. Surprisingly, only three jurisdictions (Colombia, Finland and Saudi Arabia) reported that their national corporate governance code includes a definition of a company group, although, as noted below, the codes of Peru and Spain include provisions specifically applicable to group companies. Other areas of legislation cited by respondents as including a definition of company group included: tax law, banking regulations, bankruptcy law, labour legislation and competition law.

Table 1.2. Sources of definitions of company groups

	Company law/regulations	Securities law/regulations	Listing rules	National corporate governance code	Other
Argentina	●	●	○	○	●
Austria	●	○	○	○	○
Belgium	●	○	○	○	○
Brazil	●	○	○	○	○
Chile	○	●	○	○	○
Colombia	●	○	○	●	●
Costa Rica	○	●	○	○	●
Czech Republic	●	○	○	○	○
Estonia	●	○	○	○	●
Finland	●	●	●	●	●
France	●	○	○	○	○
Germany	●	○	○	○	○
Greece	○	●	○	○	●
Hong Kong, China	●	○	●	○	○
India	●	●	○	○	○
Indonesia	○	●	○	○	○
Ireland	●	○	○	○	●
Israel	○	●	○	○	○
Japan	●	●	●	○	○
Korea	●	○	●	○	●
Latvia	○	○	○	○	●
Lithuania	○	○	○	○	●
Malaysia	●	●	○	○	○
Mexico	○	●	○	○	○
Netherlands	●	○	○	○	○
New Zealand	●	●	●	○	○
Norway	●	●	○	○	○
Peru	○	●	○	○	○
Poland	●	●	○	○	●
Portugal	●	●	○	○	○
Saudi Arabia	●	●	●	●	○
Singapore	●	○	●	○	○
Slovak Republic	●	●	○	○	○
Slovenia	●	○	○	○	●
South Africa	●	○	○	○	○
Spain	●	●	○	○	●
Sweden	●	○	○	○	○
Turkey	●	○	○	○	○
United Kingdom	●	●	●	○	○
United States	○	●	●	○	○
Canada	○	○	○	○	○
China	○	○	○	○	○
Italy	○	○	○	○	○
Russia	○	○	○	○	○
Switzerland	○	○	○	○	○
Total number of jurisdictions	**30**	**21**	**9**	**3**	**13**

Source: OECD Survey.

Virtually all explicit and implicit definitions of a company group rely heavily on the notion of "control", usually expressed in terms of majority shareholding, ability to appoint a majority of the board and contractual arrangements that give one company effective control of another. Some jurisdictions include within the group definition for some purposes "affiliated" or "associate" companies that might fall outside the strict definition of control. For example, Argentina distinguishes between subsidiaries (companies with a shareholder that has a sufficient number of votes to obtain the corporate will in shareholder meetings or dominant influence) and affiliated companies (companies with a single shareholder with more than 10% ownership). In India, associate companies are those over which another company exercises significant influence (defined as control of at least 20% of total voting power, or control of or participation in business decisions under an agreement). The New Zealand Exchange's listing rules include a subjective element in its definition of a (listed) company so as to include "all members of any group of companies or other entities of which the issuer is the holding company or has a controlling interest to the extent necessary to prevent the object of the rules being frustrated or avoided by the use of a separate entity".

The legal/regulatory frameworks of several jurisdictions separately identify groups that exhibit an enhanced level of integration. Colombia's national code of corporate governance's recommendations with special application to groups are intended for those groups whose members share "common purpose and strategy", not simply ultimate control. And, as discussed above, both *Konzernrecht* and the Rozenblum doctrine are intended to apply only in the case of groups that coordinate company activities to accomplish group objectives. Similarly, Italy's listing rules impose enhanced transparency and procedural safeguards on companies subject to "direction and coordination" by another entity.

Limitations on permissible group structures (e.g., cross- and circular shareholding, limits on layering)

Historical, economic, political, institutional, socio-cultural, legal/regulatory and other factors combine to influence the nature, prevalence and ownership and control patterns of company groups in a given jurisdiction. And while a number of reporting jurisdictions, including Israel and Korea, described important changes to group structures following legal/regulatory interventions, even these cases evidence marked path dependence. For example, in contrast to its neighbour the United States, Mexico's tax laws have historically incentivised the creation of company groups by generally minimizing taxation of the same income at both the subsidiary and parent levels. But while changes in the tax regime earlier in the 2010s removed much of the tax benefits for groups, Mexico's corporate structure remains overwhelmingly dominated by company groups.

Practically all legal/regulatory regimes effectively ban circular shareholding (where a subsidiary is the ultimate owner of shares of its parent), at least in listed companies. Cross-ownership, where companies have important interests in each other without rising to the level of parent/subsidiary, remain common in some markets and have been the subject of increasing scrutiny. As described in the Korean case study, policy makers in that jurisdiction have waged a long battle against circular and cross-share ownership, greatly reducing what had been a formerly ubiquitous practice. However, Colombia's largest economic group, Grupo Empresarial Antioqueño (GEA), remains stitched together through cross-ownership among three listed holding companies, with numerous listed subsidiaries.

Several jurisdictions volunteered information on prohibitions against common control of financial institutions and non-financial companies (mixed conglomerates). However, special legal/regulatory regimes applicable to groups of financial institutions and the treatment of cross-ownership between the financial and real sectors are outside the mandate of this report.

In their responses to the questionnaire and in the case studies that accompany this report, India and Israel highlight important recent legislation to restrict the use of pyramid structures in listed companies. As discussed in the Israel case study, that country's Law for the Promotion of Competition and Reduction of Concentration in 2013 introduced limitations on the pyramiding of listed companies that by 2020 will limit all company groups to two layers (i.e., parent and one layer of subsidiaries). In somewhat similar fashion, India's Companies Act 2013, limits company groups to two layers of subsidiaries, excluding no more than one layer of wholly-owned subsidiaries.

Transparency of group structures and operations

Together, the requirements for listed companies: (1) to prepare financial statements on a consolidated basis under IFRS; and (2) to disclose in their annual reports their major shareholders and the company's material shareholdings in other entities, serve as the core transparency provisions around company group structure and intra-group activities in virtually all jurisdictions. However, the degree of specificity required from issuers and other group companies in their disclosures around ownership, relationships among key shareholders, group structures, the role of individual companies in the group, governance policies and transparency of subsidiaries varies considerably across jurisdictions.

Principle V.A.1 recognises the inadequacy of mere technical compliance with minimum standards for disclosure of financial and operating results: "Disclosure should include, but not be limited to information on: The financial and operating results of the company." The annotation to this Principle elaborates that "[a]rguably, failures of governance can often be linked to the failure to disclose the 'whole picture'" of relations and activities within a company group.

Ownership, voting rights, shareholder agreements and director shareholdings

Principle V.A.3 recognises the fundamental importance of transparency around share ownership and corporate control: "Disclosure should include, but not be limited to, material information on: Major share ownership, including beneficial owners, and voting rights." Without a full understanding of what parties have interests in and influence over the company, and how such parties may bring their influence to bear, shareholders and markets cannot effectively predict corporate behaviour and place a value on the company's shares and other obligations.

Table 1.3. Mandatory and/or voluntary disclosure provisions for all listed companies

Number of Jurisdictions	Major share ownership	Beneficial (ultimate) owners	Corporate group structures	Special voting rights	Shareholder agreements	Cross shareholdings	Shareholdings of directors
Mandatory to the regulator/authorities only	1	7			2	1	3
Mandatory to the regulator/authorities and voluntary to public	1	3	1	1	0		2
Mandatory to public	43	32	36	37	33	22	36
Voluntary to public		2	1		2	1	3
None		1	7	7	8	21	1
Total Number of Jurisdictions	**45**	**45**	**45**	**45**	**45**	**45**	**45**

Source: OECD Survey.

The questionnaire responses tabulated in Table 1.3 evidence strong consensus around the importance of mandatory disclosure of major share ownership, special voting rights, corporate group structures and directors' shareholdings. However, there are still significant outlier jurisdictions. Czech Republic and South Africa report that listed companies in their jurisdiction are not required to publicly disclose the identity of major share owners. Corporate group structures need not be publicly disclosed in nine reporting jurisdictions, and cross shareholdings need not be disclosed in 22 (See Table 1.4). Directors' shareholdings are not required to be publicly disclosed in nine jurisdictions. There is clearly scope remaining to enhance public disclosure requirements in these areas in a significant number of responding jurisdictions.

It is difficult or impossible to fully understand what motivates a company's direction and control without the ability to identify who stands behind the owners of record of its shares. Notwithstanding, 14 jurisdictions reported that public disclosure of beneficial ownership of listed companies is not mandatory. In their responses, Ireland and Norway reported that transparency of beneficial ownership in those jurisdictions will soon be enhanced through the establishment of a central registry of beneficial owners.[13] Of course, policing of the accuracy of beneficial ownership can be exceedingly difficult, especially in the case of cross-border shareholding. Chilean rules provide that if a foreign shareholder cannot be identified with specificity, it will be presumed to be acting together with the largest shareholder.

Requirements to publicly disclose shareholder agreements and cross-shareholdings are similarly less-than-universal. Transparency around shareholder agreements is not mandatory in 14 responding jurisdictions. Agreements among large shareholders in listed companies impact incentives and thereby the behaviour of their signatories and the directors they elect to the board. Mandatory public disclosure of such agreements therefore is essential in the case of listed companies. Providing for such agreements to be null and void in the absence of public disclosure has proven an effective means of enforcement in several jurisdictions.

Table 1.4. Mandatory and/or voluntary disclosure provisions for all listed companies

	Major share ownership	Beneficial (ultimate) owners	Corporate group structures	Special voting rights	Shareholder agreements	Cross shareholdings	Shareholdings of directors
Argentina	●	■	●	●	●	-	■
Austria	●	■	●	●	-	-	●
Belgium	●	●	●	●	●	-	●
Brazil	●	●	●	●	●	-	■
Canada	●	●	●	●	●	●	●
Chile	●	●	●	●	●	-	●
China	●	●	●	●	●	-	●
Colombia	●	●	▲	●	●	●	●
Costa Rica	●	■	-	-	●	-	■
Czech Republic	■	■	●	-	-	-	◆
Estonia	●	●	●	●	●	●	●
Finland	●	●	●	●	●	-	●
France	●	■	●	-	●	-	●
Germany	●	●	●	●	●	●	●
Greece	●	■	●	●	■	■	●
Hong Kong, China	●	●	●	●	●	-	●
India	●	●	●	●	●	●	●
Indonesia	●	●	●	-	-	-	●
Ireland	●	●	-	●	●	●	●
Israel	●	●	●	-	●	●	●
Italy	●	●	●	●	●	●	●
Japan	●	◆	◆	●	◆	●	●
Korea	●	●	●	●	●	●	●
Latvia	●	●	-	●	●	-	-
Lithuania	●	◆	●	●	●	-	●
Malaysia	●	●	●	-	-	-	●
Mexico	●	●	●	●	●	●	●
Netherlands	●	●	●	●	●	-	●

	Major share ownership	Beneficial (ultimate) owners	Corporate group structures	Special voting rights	Shareholder agreements	Cross shareholdings	Shareholdings of directors
New Zealand	●	●	●	●	●	●	●
Norway	●	●	●	●	●	●	●
Peru	●	●	●	●	◆	●	◆
Poland	●	-	●	●	●	●	●
Portugal	●	●	●	●	●	●	●
Russia	●	●	●	●	●	●	●
Saudi Arabia	●	▲	●	●	●	-	●
Singapore	●	●	-	●	●	●	●
Slovak Republic	●	▲	●	▲	■	◆	▲
Slovenia	●	●	●	●	●	●	●
South Africa	▲	▲	-	●	●	-	▲
Spain	●	●	●	●	●	-	●
Sweden	●	■	-	●	-	●	●
Switzerland	●	●	●	●	-	-	◆
Turkey	●	●	-	●	-	●	●
United Kingdom	●	●	●	-	-	-	●
United States	●	●	●	●	●	●	●

●	Mandatory to public
◆	Voluntary to public
■	Mandatory to the regulator/authorities only
▲	Mandatory to the regulator/authorities and voluntary to public
-	None

Source: OECD Survey.

Group structures, governance policies and transparency of subsidiaries

Group structures typically involve the tiering of companies under an apex parent or holding company (which itself is very often controlled by an individual, family, the state or other identifiable controller). However, such structures can be complicated by pyramiding, cross-shareholding, block holding and multi-class shares. A chart laying out the shareholding relationships between group companies can be a useful way to convey the basic structure of the group, but no mere graphic representation can capture the texture and totality of the relationships among group companies. Recognising the limitations of bare-bones descriptions of group structures, the Winter Report[14] recommended that a parent company be required in its public disclosures to tell a detailed and coherent story of the group's structure and the relations among group companies.

Figure 1.2 shows that most responding jurisdictions reported that their legal/regulatory framework contains mandatory or voluntary disclosure provisions for parent companies about governance structures (32), governance policies (32) and transparency of subsidiaries (37). However, most respondents seem to be referring to the general requirements for listed companies to disclose material information on their own governance and the rules for consolidated financial reporting (e.g., Argentina: "CNV Rules enumerate[s] among others, certain elements and data be informed to CNV as relevant facts.... Among these can be included shareholding ... and group structure resulting").

Figure 1.2. Disclosure provisions of listed parent/holding companies

45 jurisdictions	Disclosure provisions exist	Disclosure provisions do not exist
Governance structures	32	13
Governance policies	32	13
Transparency of their subsidiaries	37	8

Source: OECD Survey.

The laws/regulations of some jurisdictions make more specific references to the obligation of a company that is part of a group to include in its disclosure the structure and membership in the group, the ownership relationships and (sometimes) the jurisdiction of incorporation. For example, Switzerland's *Directive on Information relating to Corporate Governance* requires issuers to describe their operational group structure, including the identity of listed and unlisted members of the group.

Requirements under the securities rules in most Canadian provinces for disclosing board diversity of listed companies also apply to their subsidiaries. Currently, all major subsidiaries of non-venture issuers must disclose statistics and policies relating to female participation on the board and in management. For listed companies subject to federal corporate legislation, disclosure requirements also include "visible minorities, disabled persons and Indigenous Canadians".

Relationship reporting; special group reporting

Five jurisdictions (Colombia, Czech Republic, Latvia, Slovenia and Turkey) reported that a company that is a member of a group may be required to publish in a special report the key aspects of its relationship with other group companies. Boards of companies that belong to a group in Colombia are explicitly required to annually prepare and present to their respective shareholders a detailed report laying out transactions between the parent and subsidiary, transactions undertaken by the parent with third parties that impact the subsidiary, and decisions that the parent or the subsidiary have taken in the interest of the other. Companies operating under one of the special regimes for companies in groups described in Part I of this chapter typically must comply with this sort of requirement.

Several other jurisdictions indicated that significant aspects of group relations would be expected to be explained in annual reports and/or required reporting on compliance with national codes of corporate governance. For example, the disclosure provisions of the section of the Italian Civil Code that permit group companies to pursue the interests of the group as a whole require disclosure (which can be in any corporate document issued by the subsidiary) of how the company was subject to the direction and coordination with the parent company. The Spanish Corporate Governance Code provides that in cases where both the parent and subsidiary are listed, the companies provide detailed disclosure on the activities they engage in and any dealings between them or between the listed subsidiary and other group companies and the mechanisms in place for resolving possible conflicts of interest.

No jurisdiction reported any legal or regulatory requirement to provide detailed information on the governance structure or governance model of subsidiaries of listed companies, or of other unlisted companies in a group to which they belong. Russia seems to have gone the farthest (though not very far) in the direction of unlisted subsidiary governance transparency. Under the Bank of Russia's regulations, an issuer must provide for each significant controlled entity: the composition of the board of directors and its members' shareholding in the controlling company; the composition of the management board and its share in the controlling company; and the identity of the CEO and his/her share in the controlling company.

The greater responsibility of parent company directors for group governance under the self-regulatory approaches of Colombia, India, Japan and Spain described at the end of Part I probably carries with it an implied obligation (or at least an expectation) of greater transparency with respect to the governance structures of unlisted companies within the group. These four jurisdictions, and others that may take a similar approach, need to ensure consistency and complementarity between the rules and expectations around parent company board responsibility for the governance of subsidiaries, on the one hand, and the disclosure regime, on the other. This may require extending reporting requirements to non-listed group members with respect to not just transactions impacting the group or its listed members, but also their own governance structures.

Composition, structure and functioning of boards and committees (and management)

Twenty-one respondents reported special requirements related to board structure and composition for company group members. However, most of these relate to the special duties of independent directors to review, report and/or decide on related-party transactions.

Substantive differences cited in the questionnaire responses between the rules around the structure and composition of boards and the requirements for directors applicable to group companies, on the one hand, and stand-alone firms, on the other, included:

a. exemption from the limitations on how many boards a director can serve on in the case of boards of companies in the same group (France; Turkey).
b. exemption from the prohibition on serving as managing director of more than one public company in the case of a parent and subsidiary (France).
c. exemption from the requirement to constitute an audit committee when the parent company's board already has one (France; Latvia; Norway, in the case of wholly-owned subsidiaries).
d. prohibition on a member of an audit committee of a listed company serving on the board of another company in the group (Israel).
e. requirements for the establishment of group-wide audit and risk committees (discussed below).

Jurisdictions with two-tiered board systems reported special treatment for company groups around composition of supervisory boards. Latvia, Lithuania and Poland impose limitations on members of the supervisory board of a parent serving on the management board of a subsidiary and the reverse. Norway's Public Limited Liability Companies Act provides that in the case of companies subject to co-determination, "it may be agreed that the employees of the whole group shall be regarded as employees of the [holding] company". This can be achieved either by agreement of the company with labour representatives or upon the order of the Ministry of Labour and Social Affairs upon request of the company or employees.

Table 1.5. Special requirements / limitations / implications for company groups with respect to certain features surveyed

	Requirements for board structure and composition	Limitations or special requirements:		Implications for whether a director is classified as "independent" when director serves on multiple boards
		For directors serving on multiple boards	For directors serving in management positions	
Argentina	○	○	○	●
Austria	○	●	●	●
Belgium	●	○	○	●
Brazil	○	○	○	●
Canada	○	○	●	●
Chile	●	●	●	●
China	○	○	●	○
Colombia	●	●	●	●
Costa Rica	●	○	○	○
Czech Republic	○	○	○	○
Estonia	●	●	○	○
Finland	○	●	●	●
France	○	●	●	○
Germany	○	●	●	●
Greece	●	○	○	●
Hong Kong, China	●	●	○	●
India	●	●	●	●
Indonesia	○	●	●	●
Ireland	●	●	●	●
Israel	●	●	●	●
Italy	●	○	○	●
Japan	●	●	●	●
Korea	●	●	●	●
Latvia	●	●	●	●
Lithuania	○	●	○	●
Malaysia	○	○	○	○
Mexico	○	○	○	●
Netherlands	○	○	○	●
New Zealand	○	●	●	●
Norway	●	●	●	●
Peru	○	○	○	●
Poland	●	●	●	○
Portugal	●	●	●	●
Russia	○	○	○	●
Saudi Arabia	●	●	●	●
Singapore	○	●	●	●
Slovak Republic	○	○	○	○
Slovenia	○	●	●	○
South Africa	○	○	●	○
Spain	●	●	●	●
Sweden	○	○	○	○
Switzerland	●	●	●	●
Turkey	○	●	●	●
United Kingdom	○	●	●	●
United States	●	●	●	●
Total number of jurisdictions	**21**	**28**	**28**	**34**

Source: OECD Survey.

Independent directors

Principles V.A.5 and VI.E do not take a position on whether an independent director on the board of a subsidiary must have no affiliation (including as an independent director) on the board of a parent or other group company. However, directors who serve concurrently on multiple boards in a company group inevitably face potential conflicts. Fifteen jurisdictions reported that a director can be classified as independent even if he or she serves as an independent director on another group company's board. Seventeen reported that an independent director on a parent company's board cannot qualify as independent on the board of a subsidiary. The remaining jurisdictions generally indicated that, while qualifying as independent on more than one group company board was not clearly prohibited, the extra scrutiny required to assess such director's independence would likely disqualify any director who serves on a parent company's board from being classified as an independent director on the board of a subsidiary.

As noted above, India affirmatively requires that an independent director of a listed company serve on the Board of an unlisted material subsidiary (20% of consolidated income or net worth).

Parent company board responsibility for oversight and governance of the group

All but nine responding jurisdictions reported the existence of special provisions related to duties of boards of companies that are members of a company group. As presented in Table 1.6, company laws and regulations are the most common source of such special provisions (29), followed by national codes of corporate governance (11), securities laws and regulations (10) and listing rules (6). Accounting laws (Czech Republic, Latvia, Poland), competition laws (Israel, Korea) and commercial codes (Spain) were the other sources of special rules cited in the responses.

Many of the jurisdictions that reported special provisions related to the duties of directors in company groups referred in their responses to the general rules around conflicts of interest, including recusal of directors from decisions in which they, or the (parent) company that appointed them, have an interest, and the special procedures and reports required for approval of such related-party transactions.

A few jurisdictions reported specific legal/regulatory requirements with respect to parent company responsibility for certain aspects of the governance of subsidiaries. India's Listing Obligations and Disclosure Requirements imposes an affirmative obligation on the audit committee of a listed parent company to review the financial statements and investments made by unlisted subsidiaries, and on the Board of the listed parent company to review the significant transactions and arrangements entered into by unlisted subsidiaries. Italy's Securities Law includes a requirement that all listed companies issue an annual Corporate Governance Report, detailing the extent of the company's adoption of the national code of corporate governance. The provision makes reference to specific code recommendations that the board of the parent evaluate the adequacy of the organisational, administrative and accounting structure of the issuer and its strategically significant subsidiaries. Its references to the board's oversight of internal controls and risk management extend to subsidiaries as well.

Several responding jurisdictions reported that their national codes of corporate governance implicitly or explicitly lay responsibility for oversight of certain group-wide activities at the feet of the parent company board. The approach taken by Colombia's code has already been noted. Ireland's national code of corporate governance (the UK Code together with the Irish Annex) provides that the board of a listed parent company "should ensure that there is adequate co-operation within the group to enable it to discharge its governance responsibilities under the Code effectively. This includes the communication of the parent company's purpose, value and strategy". It would be a reasonable interpretation that governance policies and practices of all the companies in the group would fall within this recommendation.

Table 1.6. Special provisions that address the duties of parent/holding company and subsidiary boards in company groups

	Company law/regulations	Securities law/regulations	Listing rules	National corporate governance code	Other
Argentina	●	●	○	○	○
Brazil	●	○	○	○	○
Canada	●	○	○	○	○
Chile	●	○	○	○	○
China	○	○	○	●	○
Colombia	●	○	○	●	○
Costa Rica	○	●	○	○	○
Czech Republic	●	○	○	○	●
Finland	●	○	●	○	○
France	●	●	○	○	○
Germany	●	○	○	○	○
Greece	●	○	○	●	○
Hong Kong, China	●	○	●	○	○
India	●	●	●	○	○
Indonesia	○	●	○	○	○
Ireland	●	○	○	●	○
Israel	●	●	○	○	○
Italy	●	●	○	●	○
Japan	●	○	○	●	○
Korea	●	○	○	○	●
Latvia	●	○	○	○	○
Lithuania	○	○	○	●	○
Netherlands	●	○	○	○	○
New Zealand	●	○	●	○	○
Norway	●	○	○	○	○
Poland	●	●	○	○	●
Portugal	●	○	○	○	○
Russia	○	○	○	●	○
Saudi Arabia	●	○	○	○	○
Slovak Republic	○	○	○	●	○
Slovenia	●	○	○	○	○
South Africa	●	○	○	○	○
Spain	●	○	○	●	○
Turkey	●	●	○	○	○
United Kingdom	○	○	●	●	○
United States	●	●	●	○	○
Austria	○	○	○	○	○
Belgium	○	○	○	○	○
Estonia	○	○	○	○	○
Malaysia	○	○	○	○	○
Mexico	○	○	○	○	○
Peru	○	○	○	○	○
Singapore	○	○	○	○	○
Sweden	○	○	○	○	○
Switzerland	○	○	○	○	○
Total number of jurisdictions	**29**	**10**	**6**	**11**	**3**

Source: OECD Survey.

The Russian Corporate Governance Code explicitly tasks the parent company and its board with responsibility for group-wide (parent company and controlled legal entities) policy and operations in several areas including:

a. strategy and performance evaluation
b. organisation of business processes and responsibilities
c. powers of the parent company's board to select the directors of subsidiary board
d. board member share ownership

Russia's code recommends a separate structural unit for risk management and internal controls whose ambit would extend to companies under its control.

As governance risk becomes a greater focus of attention of market participants, regulators, standard setters and companies, more jurisdictions can be expected to debate whether to assign greater responsibility to parent company boards for understanding and driving the governance systems of subsidiaries.

Audit and control environment

Figure 1.3. Special requirements with respect to certain audit features at the subsidiary and parent/holding company levels

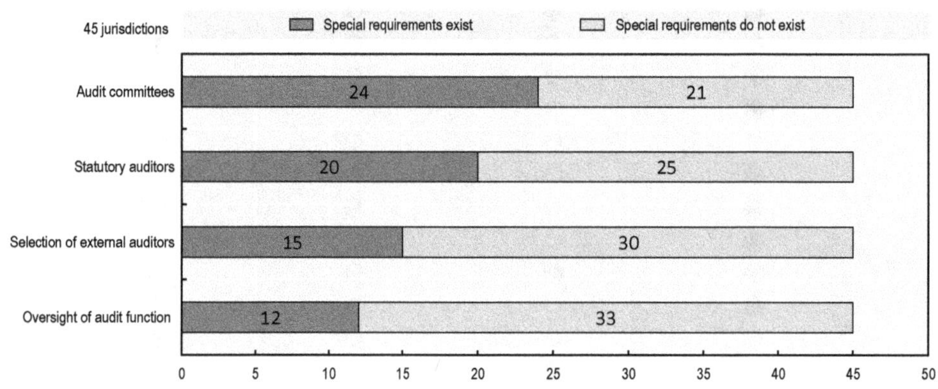

Source: OECD Survey.

Several responding jurisdictions referred to the imperative of preparing consolidated financial statements as an important driver for the implicit responsibility of parent company boards for the adequacy of the group-wide audit and control environment. However, expectations around the level of coordination and oversight required by the parent company board and management appear to vary. Colombia's national code of corporate governance seems to go the furthest by explicitly assigning the board of the parent company responsibility for the group's control architecture and approach to risk management, and the parent's CRO with responsibility for execution of group-wide risk management.

Responses to the questionnaire also evidenced diversity around the approach to auditor selections. Peru's national code of corporate governance recommends that the external auditors of the parent company in a company group should also serve as the auditors of all group companies, including those organised or operating abroad. Costa Rican regulations require that all domestic members of a financial conglomerate share the same audit firm.

Other respondents appear to be less forceful in their expectations around group-wide auditing and controls, with the auditors of the parent company (and by extension the audit committee and board of the parent company that oversee the audit process) required only to take responsibility for the audit of the consolidated statements and to reasonably ensure that the auditors of the subsidiaries, if different, have conducted their audits appropriately. The auditors of an Indian listed company are likewise required to undertake a limited review of the audits of consolidated entities. Notably, the separate audited financial statements of each subsidiary of an Indian listed company must be disclosed on the listed company's website.

Risk management and oversight

The discussions in the responses indicate that, in most reporting jurisdictions, the general duties of directors to oversee risk management probably encompass at least some measure of oversight of risks to which material subsidiaries and other group companies may be exposed. Some respondents made reference to the board's duty to provide in the annual report a faithful picture of the company and the risks it faces. However, over 40% (19) of all respondents reported that they do not have any explicit requirement for the board of a parent company to oversee, monitor and/or evaluate systems and policies related to risk management within the group distinct from the general requirements of oversight for the company itself (See Table 1.7.).

Some statutory descriptions of the obligation of the board to oversee risk specifically refer to subsidiary companies. Japan's Company Act assigns the board responsibility for the adequacy of "systems to ensure the propriety of business activities in a group of enterprises comprised of the relevant stock company and any Parent Company and Subsidiary Companies thereof". Korea's listing rules specify that an issuer's obligation to disclose financial and operational risks extend to the financial condition and key business operation of subsidiaries. Chile's response to the questionnaire notes that the general "comply or explain" framework of rules on corporate governance issued by its securities regulator explicitly include "sustainability, economic, social and environment risks" as within the ambit of the board's duty and the general materiality standards under Chilean law would extend the duty to oversight of such risks across the group.

The EU's Non-Financial Disclosure Directive (2014/95/EU) is explicit in applying on a group-wide basis its requirements for disclosure of information on the way "large undertakings and groups" operate and manage social and environmental risk. Its provisions are intended to require "[p]ublic-interest entities which are parent undertakings of a large group exceeding on its balance sheet dates, on a consolidated basis, the criterion of the average number of 500 employees during the financial year" to publish "a consolidated non-financial statement containing information to the extent necessary for an understanding of the group's development, performance, position and impact of its activity, relating to, as a minimum, environmental, social and employee matters, respect for human rights, anti-corruption and bribery matters". The Directive itself is flexible with respect to what reporting framework / guidelines companies may employ to organise and present such information, with member states free to provide more detailed requirements or more specific reporting guidance. The Directive went into effect for financial reporting years beginning at or after 1 January 2017. All member states have completely or substantially transposed the Directive into national law.[15] The questionnaire responses of Belgium, Ireland, Italy and Spain made specific reference to such companies' national legislation implementing the Directive. Greece's response noted that a listed company's corporate governance statement must cover the governance structures of all entities in the consolidation. This includes disclosure on the key features of the internal control and risk management systems of all entities in the consolidation.

Table 1.7. Explicit requirements to oversee, monitor and/or evaluate the implementation systems and policies within the group related to risk management of certain risks

	Financial risks	Operational risks	Compliance risks	Sustainability risks	Supply chain due diligence risks	Market risks
Argentina	●	●	●	●	●	●
Belgium	●	●	●	●	●	●
Canada	●	-	-	-	-	-
Chile	●	●	●	●	-	●
China	●	●	●	●	●	●
Colombia	■	■	■	-	■	■
Costa Rica	■	■	■	-	-	■
Finland	●	●	●	▲	-	●
France	-	■	■	■	■	-
Greece	●	●	●	-	-	●
Hong Kong, China	●	●	●	●	●	●
India	▲	▲	▲	▲	▲	▲
Ireland	●	●	●	●	●	●
Italy	●	●	●	●	●	●
Japan	●	●	●	●	●	●
Korea	▲	■	■	-	-	-
Malaysia*	■	■	■	-	-	-
Netherlands	●	●	●	●	-	-
Peru	●	●	●	●	●	●
Portugal	-	-	-	■	-	-
Singapore	■	■	■	■	■	■
Slovak Republic	●	●	●	-	●	●
Slovenia	●	●	●	●	●	●
Spain	▲	▲	▲	▲	▲	-
United Kingdom	■	■	■	■	■	■
Austria	-	-	-	-	-	-
Brazil	-	-	-	-	-	-
Czech Republic	-	-	-	-	-	-
Estonia	-	-	-	-	-	-
Germany	-	-	-	-	-	-
Indonesia	-	-	-	-	-	-
Israel	-	-	-	-	-	-
Latvia	-	-	-	-	-	-
Lithuania	-	-	-	-	-	-
Mexico	-	-	-	-	-	-
New Zealand	-	-	-	-	-	-
Norway	-	-	-	-	-	-
Poland	-	-	-	-	-	-
Russia	-	-	-	-	-	-
Saudi Arabia	-	-	-	-	-	-
South Africa	-	-	-	-	-	-
Sweden	-	-	-	-	-	-
Switzerland	-	-	-	-	-	-
Turkey	-	-	-	-	-	-
United States	-	-	-	-	-	-

●	Only pursuant to duties of directors under provisions of general application
■	Only pursuant to provisions of special application to company groups and their member companies
▲	Both
-	None

Information flows within the company group

As discussed in the introduction, reduction of informational asymmetries and sharing of knowledge and expertise are among the principal justifications for the existence of company groups. Access to information from subsidiaries is clearly important for the parent board's ability to arrive at and implement common policies and pursue common group-wide objectives. Obstacles to access to key information on the activities of group companies can impede the ability of directors to fulfil their fiduciary duties to shareholders and carry out other responsibilities assigned to parent company boards. So it is perhaps surprising that the questionnaire responses indicate that the black letter law of most responding jurisdictions does not provide a parent company special rights to request and receive information from a subsidiary that is not available to other shareholders.

Perhaps one of the reasons few legal frameworks appear to accord special information rights within company groups is a reluctance to introduce exceptions to the general principle of equality of shareholder rights. Several respondents noted that like other shareholders, parent companies and their directors and officers have certain inspection rights that permit them to examine the books and records of the company under certain circumstances.

However, there are clearly exceptions to the general pattern of legal parity of parent companies and other shareholders when it comes to access to information. Chile presents a quite special case of privilege accorded parent company rights to information on subsidiaries. Chilean legislation explicitly empowers board members of a parent company to examine the books and records of its subsidiaries and "to attend any board meeting of a subsidiary with voice but no vote". While not going as far as Chile's, Norway's company law explicitly provides that the board of a subsidiary is required to provide information requested by the board of the parent company, and that the board of the parent may receive information not available to other shareholders. Belgium reported case law suggesting that a director's right to information reaches to the company's subsidiary. Belgian courts derive this right from the director's responsibility to effectively carry out his/her fiduciary duties to the company, including in particular, the responsibility of the board to ensure the accuracy of the annual report and financial statements.

As noted earlier, Colombia's national code of corporate governance includes a recommendation that the parent company and important subsidiaries enter into and publish a framework for institutional relations that lay out, inter alia, the responsibilities of directors and officers for handling information among the entities in the group.

Several questionnaire respondents emphasised that rules regarding treatment of material non-public (privileged) information (MNPI) apply equally in the context of company groups. A subsidiary company's directors and managers have a duty to restrict MNPI to those with legitimate need for it and directors and officers of a company with access to MNPI regarding another group company would ordinarily be classified as "insiders" for purposes of insider trading laws.

With the exceptions of Germany and Norway, no responding jurisdictions reported that a subsidiary may require its parent to share information about itself or another group company. Germany reported that within the non-Control Agreement *Konzernrecht* framework "the directors of the controlled company have the right and obligation to demand detailed information as to the solvency of the controlling company" in order to assess the controlling company's ability to effect any compensation it will ultimately have to make to the subsidiary.[16] Norway's law includes a provision requiring the parent company to inform the board of a subsidiary prior to final adoption of matters and resolutions by the parent company that may be of importance to the subsidiary. This provision is consistent with the principle of Norwegian company law that it is ultimately the general assembly that governs the corporation, and hence the general assembly of a subsidiary must be equipped with all information material to the decisions it makes for the company.

Table 1.8. Specific rights / obligations / provisions / exception for company groups

Number of Jurisdictions	Only pursuant to duties of directors under provisions of general application	Only pursuant to provisions of special application to company groups and their member companies	Both	No rights/ provisions/ exceptions
The right or the obligation to request and receive non-public information from other entities in the group, including the parent/holding company	16	6	6	17
Provisions of law or regulation for "piercing the corporate veil" to hold a parent/holding company (or its officers or directors) accountable when the parent/holding company causes decisions to be taken at the subsidiary level that are, in fact, not in the interest of the subsidiary but rather in the interest of the parent/holding company	19	9	5	12
Exceptions to a director's fiduciary duties of loyalty and care to the company on whose board s/he serves, when the company is controlled by another enterprise	7	7	2	29

Source: OECD Survey.

Misuse of subsidiaries to avoid compliance with legal obligations of listed companies

The use of the corporate form (including subsidiary and affiliate companies and "letter box" companies) for the avoidance of compliance with the legal obligations of listed and unlisted entities has been the subject of a great deal of warranted attention and debate. In the context of the issues addressed in this report, instances of misuse of subsidiaries to carry out transactions, borrowings and other actions to the detriment of minority shareholders has been an issue of special concern in India.[17] In response, the Securities and Exchanges Board of India (SEBI) imposed a requirement unique among the jurisdictions surveyed for this report: the board of directors of unlisted subsidiaries representing 20% of consolidated income or net worth of an Indian listed company must include at least one of the independent directors of the listed parent. As explained in the India case study, the purpose of this requirement is to provide the independent director/s of the listed parent direct access to the workings of the subsidiary to ensure that the latter is not used to avoid disclosure or board, or shareholder approval requirements that would be applicable at the listed parent company level. Estonia and the United States reported that executive compensation disclosure and/or approval requirements explicitly cover employees of subsidiary companies.

Liability of parent for obligations and actions of subsidiaries

"Piercing the corporate veil" refers to instances where a court or other authority disregards the legal separation of a corporation from its shareholders, and holds the latter directly liable for the debts and obligations of the former. The questionnaire responses about piercing the corporate veil generally stressed that the most extreme form of this doctrine is limited to very exceptional cases, generally instances of establishment or operation of a subsidiary company to carry out fraud or for another malicious purpose. Canada's response cited a case affirming that the separation of entities would be ignored only when not to do so would yield a result "too flagrantly opposed to justice, convenience or the interests of Revenue". Japan applies its version of the doctrine only "when the corporate entity completely lacks substance or if the corporate entity is abused to avoid application of laws".

Of the responding jurisdictions, Colombia and China seem to be the least restrictive in the use of piercing the corporate veil as a remedy for improper acts by a subsidiary. Colombian law empowers the Superintendency of Companies (in addition to the courts) to ignore the limited liability of a parent company (as shareholder of its subsidiary) for fraudulent acts causing damage to third parties. China's questionnaire response noted that "[s]hareholder[s] must not infringe on the company's interests by abusing shareholders rights, or harm the interests of the company's creditor by abusing the independent legal status or the shareholders limited liabilities. If a shareholder of a company has caused any losses to the company or to other shareholders by abusing shareholders rights, it shall be held liable for compensation."

Another means whereby a parent company may find itself responsible for the obligations and actions of a subsidiary is the application of the *de facto* or "shadow director" concept. Applying this concept, a person or entity that in actual fact directs and controls the company (i.e., acting in the place of the company's directors or board) may be regarded as a "shadow director" and thereby subject to the same duties of loyalty and care as a *de jure* director. Responses to the questionnaire reported that in Hong Kong, China, a parent company (and its officers and directors), and In Ireland, its officers and employees in certain circumstances, can be determined to be a shadow director of its subsidiary. The Israeli Companies Law prohibits interference with a director's independent judgment and regards directors of parent companies who interfere in the management of a subsidiary as shadow directors who owe fiduciary duties to the subsidiaries. As a corollary, the Israeli Supreme Court recognised a right of shareholders to bring a derivative suit against the parent company as a shadow director of the subsidiary.

The shadow director concept is by no means alien to non-common law jurisdictions. Russia's Civil Code imposes a duty to act in a reasonable and *bona fide* manner on any person who de facto can determine the actions of the board or management of a company. Korea's Company Law specifically ascribes director liability on any "person who instructs a director to conduct business by using his/her influence over the company", which would reach the officers and directors of a parent company.

Short of completely disregarding the legal separation of parent and subsidiary, the laws of a number of responding jurisdictions clearly do assign liability to parent companies for particular types of obligations and actions of subsidiaries under certain circumstances. The most commonly cited examples in the questionnaire responses revolved around insolvency of a subsidiary due to direct mismanagement by a parent company. Irish company law provides that a court can order a parent company to help pay off the debts of a subsidiary in bankruptcy if it is "just and equitable" to do so. But this provision is interpreted as applicable only when responsibility for the bankruptcy rests with the parent. Similarly, and more apposite for directors, Czech bankruptcy law provides for liability of controlling entities in the case of breaches of duty of care resulting in bankruptcy.[18]

The Italian Civil Code allows minority shareholders (and creditors) of a subsidiary to sue for damages suffered because the parent caused the subsidiary to be operated contrary to "principles of correct company and business management". However, reflecting Italy's recognition of the group concept discussed earlier, parent companies can exert an affirmative defence that any damages were offset by other transactions or taking into account the totality of the direction and coordination.

Other instances of liability of parent companies for the obligations or actions of subsidies cited in the questionnaire responses relate to areas of particular stakeholder concern and typically derive from legislation outside the national company and securities law framework:

a. Labour and worker safety legislation: French labour law includes the concept of co-employment, which can extend responsibility to the parent company for the dismissal of employees of subsidiaries. New Zealand's response noted "[t]here are numerous other provisions of New Zealand law, of general application, under which a holding company could be found liable for the actions of subsidiaries e.g. obligations in relation to health and safety at work".
b. Environmental degradation: Finland's Law on Compensation for Environmental Damage may subject company groups and their controllers to liability for actions of subsidiaries.
c. Corruption and bribery: Ireland's response highlighted instances where Irish regulators and courts can impose liability on parent companies for a subsidiary's breach of law related to environmental damage, health and safety and bribery.[19]

The examples provided above highlight the real potential for unlimited liability of parent companies for obligations and actions of subsidiaries, even in the absence of "piercing the corporate veil" or cases of abuse of the corporate form. Nonetheless, some parent company boards may be reluctant to take on greater responsibility for group company activities in these areas over concern that doing so would be viewed as acknowledgement of the parent company's ultimate liability. Future research in this area might examine how company group practices and boards have adjusted to take into account the particular exposure of parent companies in cases of subsidiary violations of labour, environmental and anti-corruption legislation.

References

Brett, Alan (2019), "Assessing Control: Measuring the alignment between economic exposure and voting power at controlled companies". MSCI ESG Research LLC, https://www.msci.com/documents/10199/a7c17b59-10de-9849-9f7c-1f70abece5da.

Cohen, Zipora (1991), "Fiduciary Duties of Controlling Shareholders: A Comparative View". University of Pennsylvania Journal of International Business Law, Vol. 12:3, pp. 379-410.

Conac, Pierre-Henri (2016), "The Chapter on Groups of Companies of the European Model Company Act (EMCA)". European Company and Financial Law Review, Vol. 13:2, pp. 301–321.

Enterprise 2020 CSR Europe, GRI and Accountancy Europe (2018), *Member State Implementation of Directive 2014/95/EU: A Comprehensive Overview of How Member States Are Implementing the EU Directive on Nonfinancial and Diversity Information, 2018.*

European Commission (2002), *Report of the High Level Group of Company Law Experts on a Modern Regulatory Framework for Company Law in Europe* ("Winter Report").

European Model Company Act (2015), Chapter 15 "Groups of Companies".

Informal Company Law Expert Group (2016), *Report on the Recognition of the Interest of the Group*.

Institutional Investor Advisory Services (2014), "Unlisted Subsidiaries: The New Cloaking Device".

Latin American Companies Circle (2014), "Corporate Governance Recommendations for Company Groups".

Ministry of Economy, Trade and Industry, Japan (2019), "Provisional Guidelines for Group Governance System". Presentation, provisional translation.

OECD (2019a), *Owners of the World's Listed Companies*, Paris.

OECD (2019b), *OECD Corporate Governance Factbook*, Paris.

OECD (2018), *Flexibility and Proportionality in Corporate Governance*, Paris.

OECD (2017), *Corporate Governance in Colombia*, Paris.

OECD (2015a), *G20/OECD Principles of Corporate Governance*, OECD Publishing, Paris, https://doi.org/10.1787/9789264236882-en.

OECD (2015b), *Corporate Governance of Company Groups in Latin America*, Paris.

OECD (2013), *Supervision and Enforcement in Corporate Governance*, Paris.

OECD (2012), *Latin America Corporate Governance Roundtable Task Force Report on Related Party Transactions*, Paris.

OECD (2012), *Related Party Transactions and Minority Shareholder Rights*, Paris.

OECD (2009), *Guide to Fighting Abusive Related Party Transactions in Asia*, Paris.

Sørenson, Karsten Engsig (2018), "The Duties and Responsibilities of Boards in Company Groups". Report for OECD Corporate Governance Committee, DAF/CA/CG(2018)11.

Winner, Martin (2016), "Group Interest in European Company Law: an Overview". Acta Univ. Sapientiae, Vol. 5:1, pp. 85-96.

Notes

[1] Treatment of related-party transactions has also been an almost universal focus of attention. An outline of the Committee's considerable previous work on this topic, both within and outside the context of company groups, is provided later in this publication.

[2] Brett, Alan, *Assessing control: Measuring the alignment between economic exposure and voting power at controlled companies*, MSCI ESG Research, April 2019.

[3] OECD (2012), *Related Party Transactions and Minority Shareholder Rights*, p.11.

[4] *Practical Guidelines for Group Governance System*, provisional translation of a presentation prepared by the Corporate System Division, Economic and Industrial Policy Bureau, Ministry of Economy, Trade and Industry, Japan.

[5] Sørenson (2018), *The Duties and Responsibilities of Boards in Company Groups*, p. 5.

[6] Annotation to Principle II.G.

[7] Czech Republic's law regulating "*koncerny*" was also influenced by *Konzernrecht*, but the new Czech corporate law (2014) and subsequent case law indicate a movement away from this approach.

[8] Of course, this provision protects subsidiary directors only so long as such instructions are lawful. They remain liable for carrying out any illicit instructions of the holding company.

[9] Brazil's company law provides a similar option for related companies to enter into a specific contract to govern the relationship among members of the group. However, the Brazilian chapter of Company Groups in Latin America, prepared by Brazil's securities commission, noted that only two listed companies availed themselves of this option.

[10] Procedural considerations motivate French plaintiffs to pursue claims against directors for these sorts of alleged violations in criminal rather than civil court. Accordingly, the Rozenblum Doctrine has rarely if ever been asserted in civil cases in France itself.

[11] The term actually employed in the glossary to the Colombian code is "conglomerate".

[12] From a provisional translation of the presentation, *Practical Guidelines for Group Governance System,* provided by the Corporate System Division, Economic and Industrial Policy Bureau, METI, Japan. An English translation of the Group Guidelines is not yet available.

[13] The EU Money Laundering Directive (2015/849/EU) requires certain minimum levels of transparency of beneficial ownership in EU member states.

[14] *Report of the High Level Group of Company Law Experts on a Modern Regulatory Framework for Company Law in Europe* and the press release of the High Level Group of Company Law Experts (November 2002), both at www.europa. eu.int/comm/internal_market.

[15] For details and comparisons of how member states have transposed the Directive into national legislation, see Enterprise 2020 CSR Europe, GRI and Accountancy Europe, *Member State Implementation of Directive 2014/95/EU: A Comprehensive Overview of How Member States Are Implementing the EU Directive on Nonfinancial and Diversity* Information, 2018. http://bit.ly/2K8muhC..

[16] Germany's questionnaire response notes that such right and obligation on the part of the subsidiary's directors is established in case law rather than codified in statute.

[17] Institutional Investor Advisory Services, "Unlisted Subsidiaries: The New Cloaking Device", August 2014.

[18] Debate is ongoing in many jurisdictions around the possibility that directors and controllers may owe fiduciary duties to creditors and other stakeholders when a firm is in or near insolvency. Article 19 ("Duties of directors where there is a likelihood of insolvency") of the recent EU Directive on Preventive Restructuring Arrangements (2019/1023/EU) states that "Member States shall ensure that, where there is a likelihood of insolvency, directors, have due regard, as a minimum, to the following: (a) the interests of *creditors*, equity holders and *other stakeholders*..." [emphasis added]. The US case of *North American Catholic Education Programming Foundation, Inc. v. Gheewalla, 930 A.2d 92 (Del. 2007)* established that "The directors of an insolvent firm do not owe any particular duties to creditors. They continue to owe fiduciary duties to the corporation for the benefit of *all of its residual claimants, a category which now includes creditors*" [emphasis added].

[19] Several respondents noted that anti-competition law fines and penalties are frequently applied on a group-wide basis.

i. Questionnaire

CORPORATE GOVERNANCE THEMATIC REVIEW ON THE DUTIES AND RESPONSIBILITIES OF BOARDS IN COMPANY GROUP STRUCTURES

BACKGROUND AND GUIDE FOR FILLING IN THE QUESTIONAIRE

Background and purpose

The Financial Stability Board (FSB) has conducted a peer review on the implementation of the *G20/OECD Principles of Corporate Governance* for publicly listed regulated financial institutions. The Chair of the FSB's review team presented the preliminary results of the review to *the Corporate Governance Committee* in November 2016. The final recommendations from the FSB review were published in April 2017 and included a proposal to the OECD for a follow-up review on practices with respect to the effectiveness of rules regarding the duties, responsibilities and composition of boards within group structures.

Company groups, in which a parent/holding company controls one or more subsidiary entities, are common in both advanced and emerging markets. Company groups serve a variety of legitimate and economically beneficial purposes, including: leveraging of expertise, intellectual property and brands; achievement of business synergies; efficiency in capital structures; and compliance with national laws (especially in the case of cross-border company groups). However, company group structures may also present challenges for boards especially when beneficial ownership of the parent and subsidiary company is not identical (e.g., when the subsidiary is a listed company). And in making decisions, a director on the board of a company within the group may be expected to consider also the wider interests of the company group to which it belongs. How effectively the interests of the shareholders and other stakeholders of each company in the group are served, therefore depends on how these challenges are approached and resolved through the formulation of the duties and responsibilities of the board.

Against this background, the *Corporate Governance Committee* agreed, at its meeting in October 2018, to conduct a peer review on the *Duties and Responsibilities of Boards in Company Group Structures* and to collect information from all jurisdictions via a questionnaire sent to delegates. The results from this questionnaire will be used to present an overview of the legal/regulatory framework with respect to board duties and responsibilities and identify different approaches to tackle the common phenomena of group structures.

Scope of your answers and definitions

The main focus of the *G20/OECD Principles of Corporate Governance* ("*G20/OECD Principles*") is to provide guidance for regulation that is applicable to listed companies, regardless of whether the company is part of a group or not. At the same time, the *G20/OECD Principles* also contain several specific references to company groups that are relevant in the context of the duties of boards in company groups. This questionnaire addresses the company group-related issues that are addressed in the *G20/OECD*

Principles. The exception is related party transactions, on which extensive information is already available in the OECD Corporate Governance Factbook 2019.

What to include

In order to determine the scope of your answers, please consider that this questionnaire focuses on the corporate governance framework as it applies to all companies (listed or not) in a company group in which at least one company in the group is *publicly listed*. The relevant legal/regulatory areas to be considered in the responses ("*the legal/regulatory framework*") typically include company law, securities law, listing rules and national corporate governance codes. Established case law may also be an important source of information.

General vs. specific laws/regulations: Questions 9 through 12 ask whether there exist relevant provisions: (1) under laws and regulations of *general application to all companies*; and/or (2) under laws and regulations *specifically applicable to company groups and their member companies*. The reason for inquiring about laws and regulations that do not specifically reference company groups is that the general framework of company law and regulation very well may include provisions that address the issues raised in this questionnaire, even where company groups are not legally defined or subject to a distinct legal/regulatory regime. Accordingly, we ask that in responding to each of these questions, you be particularly mindful of provisions of the general legal/regulatory framework that may de facto govern the behaviour of members of company groups and their boards in the circumstances described in the question.

Corporate governance codes: If you refer to a national corporate governance code, please indicate if the provisions of the code you refer to are mandatory or voluntary. Code recommendations that require "comply or explain" will for the purpose of this survey be considered voluntary (even if the code includes mandatory requirements for companies to disclose their practices). Please do not consider any other voluntary codes, such as self-regulatory arrangements, voluntary commitments and business practices.

Special sectors of activity and firms: This questionnaire does not seek to collect information about legal/regulatory provisions whose application is limited to special sectors of activity, for example the financial sector, state-owned enterprises and foreign companies listed in your jurisdiction. Please exclude any sector-specific regulation in your responses.

Questionnaire

Question 1: Please indicate whether any of the following includes a specific definition of company groups:

- Company law/regulations
- Securities law/regulations
- Listing rules
- National corporate governance code
- Other laws, regulations, or case law – please specify
- None

(Response requested if your previous answer was different from "None")

Please briefly describe the definition(s) of company groups in your jurisdiction, and where such definition(s) may be found.

Please do not exceed 300 words (2000 characters)

Question 2: Does the legal/regulatory framework in general (i.e., for all listed companies, not just those in company groups) contain mandatory and/or voluntary *disclosure provisions* with respect to:

Please select one of the six options below for each field:

a. Yes, mandatory to the regulator/authorities only
b. Yes, mandatory to the regulator/authorities and voluntary to public
c. Yes, voluntary to the regulator/authorities only
d. Yes, mandatory to public
e. Yes, voluntary to public
f. None

	a	b	c	d	e	f
▪ *Major share ownership*						
▪ *Beneficial (ultimate) owners*						
▪ *Corporate group structures*						
▪ *Special voting rights*						
▪ *Shareholder agreements*						
▪ *Cross shareholdings*						
▪ *Shareholdings of directors*						

Question 3: Does the legal/regulatory framework applicable to listed parent/ holding companies contain mandatory and/or voluntary *disclosure provisions* about governance structures, governance policies and transparency of their subsidiaries?

	Yes, please briefly describe	**No**
▪ *Governance structures*		
▪ *Governance policies*		
▪ *Transparency of their*		

Question 4: Are companies that belong to a company group (parent/holding companies and subsidiaries) subject to any special requirements with respect to the board structure and/or board composition? [Note: Examples may include requirements related to the presence and special responsibilities of independent directors and board committees.]

Yes, please briefly describe

No

Question 5: Are there any limitations on, or special requirements for directors who serve on multiple boards or in management positions (including those of listed and unlisted companies) within the same company group?

	Yes, please briefly describe	**No**
▪ *For directors who serve on multiple boards*		
▪ *For directors who serve in management positions*		

Question 6: Does serving on multiple boards within the group have implications for whether a director is classified as "independent"?

Yes, please briefly describe

No

Question 7: Please indicate whether the legal/regulatory framework includes any specific provisions that address the duties of parent/holding company and subsidiary boards in company groups?

Please select all those elements of the framework that include or refer to such provisions.

- Company law/regulations
- Securities law/regulations
- Listing rules
- National corporate governance code
- Other laws, regulations or case law – please specify:___________________________________
- None

(Response requested if your previous answer was different from "None")

Please provide a brief overview of such provisions – and where they may be found – as they apply to the duties of parent/holding company and subsidiary boards in company groups.

Please do not exceed 300 words (2000 characters)

Question 8: Are listed companies that belong to a company group subject to any special requirements with respect to audit committees, statutory auditors, selection of external auditors and oversight of audit function at the subsidiary and parent/holding company levels?

	Yes, please briefly describe	**No**
▪ *Audit committees*		
▪ *Statutory auditors*		
▪ *Selection of external*		
▪ *Oversight of audit function*		

Question 9: Does the legal/regulatory framework or case law contain any exceptions to a director's fiduciary duties of loyalty and care to the company on whose board s/he serves, when the company is controlled by another enterprise? [Note: Examples may include provisions that permit parent/holding companies to require directors of subsidiaries to act in accordance with instructions, or to bypass the subsidiary board's ordinary authority.]

- Yes, pursuant to the duties of directors under provisions of general application in company and securities law/regulation, case law and/or the national corporate governance code
- Yes, pursuant to provisions of special application to company groups and their member companies in company and securities law/regulation, case law and/or the national corporate governance code
- No

(Response requested if your previous answer was "*Yes, ...*")

Please provide a brief overview of such provisions – and where they may be found – as they apply to the duties of parent/holding company and subsidiary boards in company groups.

Please do not exceed 300 words (2000 characters)

Question 10: Are there provisions of law or regulation for "piercing the corporate veil" to hold a parent/holding company (or its officers or directors) accountable when the parent/holding company causes decisions to be taken at the subsidiary level that are, in fact, not in the interest of the subsidiary but rather in the interest of the parent/holding company? [Note: One example would be when a parent/holding company (or its officers or directors) is judged to be a "shadow director" bound by the same fiduciary duties as a member of the Board of the company.]

- Yes, pursuant to the duties of directors under provisions of general application in company and securities law/regulation, case law and/or the national corporate governance code
- Yes, pursuant to provisions of special application to company groups and their member companies in company and securities law/regulation, case law and/or the national corporate governance code
- No

(Response requested if your previous answer was "*Yes, ...*")

Please provide a brief overview of such provisions – and where they may be found – as they apply to the duties of parent/holding company and subsidiary boards in company groups.

Please do not exceed 300 words (2000 characters)

Question 11: Does the board or management of a parent/holding company or subsidiary in a company group have the right or the obligation to request and receive non-public information from other entities in the group, including the parent/holding company?

- Yes, pursuant to the duties of directors under provisions of general application in company and securities law/regulation, case law and/or the national corporate governance code
- Yes, pursuant to provisions of special application to company groups and their member companies in company and securities law/regulation, case law and/or the national corporate governance code
- No

(Response requested if your previous answer was "*Yes, ...*")

Please provide a brief overview of such provisions – and where they may be found – as they apply to the duties of parent/holding company and subsidiary boards in company groups.

Please do not exceed 300 words (2000 characters)

Question 12: Are there any explicit requirements for the board of a parent/holding company to oversee, monitor and/or evaluate the implementation systems and policies within the group related to risk management of financial, operational, compliance, sustainability, supply chain due diligence and market risks? [Note: As mentioned in the Guide for Filling in the Questionnaire, above, please exclude any sector-specific laws/regulations in your responses.]

Please select one of the three options below for each field:

a. Yes, pursuant to the duties of directors under provisions of general application in company and securities law/regulation, case law and/or the national corporate governance code
b. Yes, pursuant to provisions of special application to company groups and their member companies in company and securities law/regulation, case law and/or the national corporate governance code
c. No

	a	b	c
▪ *Financial risks*			
▪ *Operational risks*			
▪ *Compliance risks*			
▪ *Sustainability risks*			
▪ *Supply chain due diligence risks*			
▪ *Market risks*			

(Response requested if any of your previous answers was “a” or “b”)

Please provide a brief overview of such provisions if you – and where they may be found – as they apply to the duties of parent/holding company and subsidiary boards in company groups?

Please do not exceed 300 words (2000 characters)

Q13: Please provide any additional information that is relevant to this questionnaire.

Please do not exceed 300 words (2000 characters)

Please identify your <u>jurisdiction</u>: ________________________

Please identify one <u>contact person</u> responsible for the responses to the questionnaire for your jurisdiction and her/his contact details, for the event that the OECD Secretariat has to get in touch with you for possible clarifications or follow up regarding your answers.

Name:	
Position:	
Institution:	
Email:	
Phone number:	

** End of the questionnaire **

2 Colombia case study

This chapter on Colombia describes the important and growing role that company groups play in the Colombian economy and especially among Colombian listed companies, with particular focus on financial conglomerates. It describes the legal framework, regulations and corporate governance code recommendations relevant to the supervision, governance, board duties and responsibilities in company groups, with particular attention to recent legal reforms, including the Financial Conglomerates Law of 2017. It references significant recent case law developments before concluding by highlighting principal issues and concerns, and challenges for future consideration.

Introduction

Since the 1990s, the Colombian financial system has gradually developed from a model of specialised financial institutions, toward the current system known as "multi-bank" model. The system promotes the provision of financial services through subsidiaries, generating economies of scale and, in turn, a greater concentration of ownership and control in the financial system.

Due to the evolution of the multi-bank model, the figure of "holding company" for financial and non-financial companies has gained greater prominence, and so-called "company groups" have become more present in the economy.

Nowadays, company groups are important participants across many sectors of the Colombian economy, and especially, Financial Conglomerates (FCs) play a large part in the country's economic activity.

Colombian groups are not only important for the domestic economy. They are also important regionally, as many of them have become Multilatina groups. This local and regional expansion of financial groups triggered the need to strengthen the regulatory and supervision framework for FCs.

In recent years, there have been important changes, especially with the issuance of Law 1870 in 2017[1] and its regulatory decrees, which raises the standards of supervision and regulation of FCs and subjects some financial holdings that were previously unregulated to Superintendencia Financiera de Colombia (SFC) supervision.

National context

Business groups in Colombia are responsible for a large share of the country's economic activity and include a highly significant number of the most important Colombian companies. Colombian company groups are not only important for the domestic economy, but also regionally, as many of them have become Multilatina groups.

The most recent study undertaken by the Superintendency of Companies[2] in 2018 gathered the following information regarding parent companies and their subsidiaries registered in Colombia[3]:

Figure 2.1. Holdings and subsidiaries in Colombia

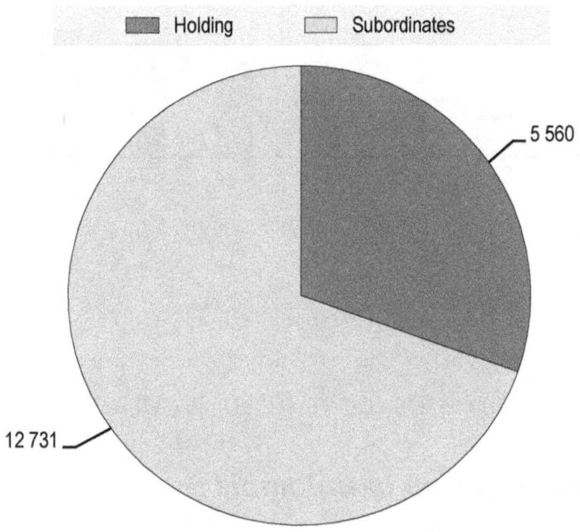

Company groups are important participants across many sectors of the Colombian economy. There are groups whose securities issuers (holdings and subsidiaries) operate in the same sector, for example, cement and construction, commerce or power generation. In such cases, the holding companies participate in their subsidiaries as investors in shares but may also directly engage in the same line of business as the subsidiary.

Colombian companies have a highly concentrated ownership structure, and most of the FCs have a pyramidal structure, although there are a few cases of cross-shareholding structures.

Company groups in Colombia have consolidated in the last ten years due to the international financial crisis of 2008/2009. Colombian FCs acquired many assets locally and in other countries in the region from international banks who found themselves obliged to retrench. Thus, the number of subsidiaries of Colombian FCs abroad increased dramatically, reaching a figure of 223 in 2019 (compared to 29 in 2006).

FCs[4] continue to be the main force behind growth in the Colombian financial system. The three largest conglomerates represent close to 60% of the total assets of the system. Large financial and mixed-activity economic groups play the dominant role among Colombia's listed companies.

In the Colombian Stock Exchange (hereinafter "BVC")[5], 53 listed companies out of 69 stock issuers (76.8%) are part of a company group; 19 of them are holding companies and 34 are subsidiaries. Among the 53 listed companies that are part of a company group, 20 of them make up 100% of the COLCAP index (which groups together Colombia's 20 largest and most liquid listed companies).

Figure 2.2. Evolution of subsidiaries abroad

Sum of individual assets (assets in millions of dollars and numbers of entities as of September 2019)

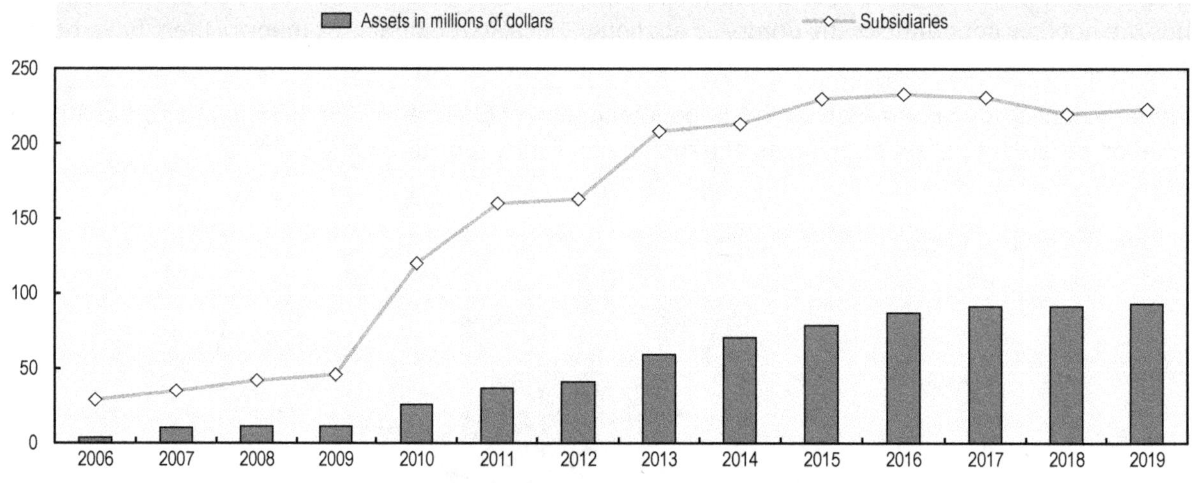

Source: SFC.
Note: Includes all subsidiaries (financial and non-financial) abroad.

Legal and regulatory developments covering company groups

Legal definitions of a company group in Colombia

In Colombia, there are several legal definitions of a company group, each with different coverage and potential implications for different companies and groups:

Law 222 of 1995 defines a corporate group based on the following three criteria:

- relationship of subordination
- unity of purpose
- management

Unity of purpose and management refer to the objective for all entities of the group gathering together to achieve a specific corporate goal set by the parent or controlling company, according to the direction they exercise on the group, without jeopardising the individual development of each company or any activities carried out by them.

The Superintendency of Companies, or when applicable, the Financial Superintendency, will establish the existence of the corporate group in the case of discrepancies (or ambiguities) regarding the originating assumptions.

Commercial law, control assumptions

The Commercial Code considers branches and subsidiaries as those entities that submit their decision-making power to another entity, which is considered a holding company. If the headquarters exercises its decision-making powers or control directly over the subordinate company, the latter will be considered a branch (*filial*). If such powers are exercised indirectly over the subordinate, the controlled entity will be considered a subsidiary.

According to the article 261 of the Commercial Code, a company is subordinated if it is in one or more of the following cases:

"When more than fifty percent (50%) of the capital belongs to the holding company, directly or through its subordinates, or the subordinates of such entities. For this purpose, shares with preferential dividend and without voting rights will not be computed.

When the holding company and subordinates have jointly or separately the right to vote by constituting the minimum decision-making majority in the board of directors or in the shareholders' assembly, or have the number of votes necessary to elect the majority of members of the board of directors.

When the holding company, directly or through its subordinates, by carrying out an act or business with the controlled company or partners, exercises influence on the decisions of the company's management bodies.

Likewise, for all legal purposes, it is subordinated when the control is exercised by one or more natural or legal persons of a non-corporate nature, either directly or through other entities, in which they own more than fifty percent (50%) of the capital or set the minimum majority for decision making or exert dominant influence in the direction or decision making of the entity".

The definition of subordination is broad, so the fundamental determinant is if the decision-making power of a company is subject to the will of one or more other persons. It is worth mentioning that the control presumptions previously indicated are not intended as exhaustive, but merely illustrative, as there may be other forms of control.

Regarding insolvency of non-financial companies, applicable regulation defines company groups as:

"Group of Companies: Groups consisting of natural persons, legal persons, or independent trusts participating in economic activities, related among themselves due to their condition of parent, controlling or subordinated companies or upon most of their capital belonging to or being under the administration of such natural or legal persons, either acting directly or through other persons or through independent trusts".

In general, the above definitions are not absolute. In each case, the authorities can review the different circumstances and can declare the existence of a group of companies.

Law 1870 of 2017 – Financial Conglomerates Law

The Law defines an FC as “a group of entities with a common controlling shareholder that includes two or more national or foreign entities that carry out an activity of the entities supervised by the SFC, provided that at least one of them exercises such activities in Colombia.

The holding company and the following subordinated entities make up FCs:

a. Entities subject to the inspection and supervision of the SFC and its national and/or foreign financial subordinates.

b. Entities abroad that exercise an activity of the entities supervised by the SFC, and its national and/or foreign financial subordinates.

c. Legal entities or investment vehicles through which the financial holding company exercises control of the entities referred to in subparagraphs (a) and (b) of this article”.

This regulation also stipulates in Article 3 that a financial holding company (FHC) is “*any legal entity or investment vehicle exercising the first level of control or significant influence over the entities that make up a financial conglomerate*”. The FHC is responsible for the compliance with the provisions of this title.

The control and subordination concepts established in Articles 260 and 261 of the Commercial Code (provisions previously specified) will be applied to the FHC. In addition, in the case of the presumption of Numeral 1 of Article 261 of the Commercial Code, ordinary shares with voting rights of those shareholders who cannot have control in accordance with the rules that govern them, shall not figure in the calculation.

Recent legal and regulatory developments covering company groups

With the issuance of the new Law of FCs, the SFC was endowed with new powers and intervention instruments that may also be exercised with respect to the parent companies (FHCs), which are not required to be financial institutions themselves or exclusively engaged in financial sector businesses.

The SFC may issue orders to an FHC related to risk management, internal control, disclosure of information, conflicts of interest and corporate governance; to be applied by the entities that make up the FC. Likewise, it may request information and make on-site inspections of the subsidiaries and even order the FHC to change the structure of the FC provided since the existing one does not allow an adequate disclosure of information or/and a comprehensive and consolidated supervision.

Among the 52 listed companies that are part of FCs in Colombia, three are companies supervised as FHCs under Law 1870 (*Grupo Sura, Grupo Aval and Grupo Bolívar*), 13 are supervised as subsidiaries (*Banco Davivienda, Banco Coomeva, Banco AV Villas, Banco Popular, Alpopular, Banco de Occidente, Banco de Bogotá, Almaviva, Corficolombiana, Bancolombia, AFP Proteccion, Tuya CFC and Banco Caja Social*) and 13 are non-financial controlled issuers related to FCs (*Promigas, Surtigas del Caribe, Gases de Occidente, Infrastructure Projects, Grupo Argos, Cementos Argos, Odinsa, Celsia, Empresa Energía del Pacífico, Empresa de Energía de Tulua, Grupo Nutresa, Suramericana and Almacenes Éxito*).

Of the COLCAP 20 companies, 11 are part of FCs, as follows:

- Two are FHCs under the terms of Law 1870 (*Grupo Aval and Grupo Sura*).
- Four are under SFC supervision, as part of FCs (*Banco de Bogotá, Banco Davivienda, Bancolombia and Corficolombiana*).
- Five non-financial securities issuers are part of FCs (*Grupo Nutresa, Cementos Argos, Grupo Argos, Celsia and Almacenes Éxito*).

All of the above companies are under SFC supervision.

In general, for all Colombian financial entities, regardless of whether they are part of a group of companies or not, the functions of the boards of directors are those established in the commercial law and other regulations in force. Some of the functions that the SFC considers key and non-delegable are:

1. actively participate in the design and approval of strategic objectives and business plans (including levels of capital and liquidity) and products
2. define the governance structure, supervise its implementation and review it periodically
3. Set the policy of selection, compensation and replacement of the most important positions, and follow up on their compliance
4. determine and implement the risk governance structure, which means to define the strategy and risk appetite, review the policies and procedures of risk management, and verify that they are met
5. supervise the administration of the Senior Management
6. monitor the Internal Control System

Another function of the board that deserves special attention from the SFC is the approval of the policies related to conflicts of interest and related party transactions (RPTs).The SFC especially verifies that the corporate governance framework of the entity or FHC contains policies covering the disclosure, approval and monitoring of operations (active, passive and neutral) in which a related party participates. Said policies must establish, *inter alia*, that these operations must be carried out at market prices and in the interest of the entity.

According to Decree 1486 of 2018[6], the board of an FHC must comply with at least the following functions and responsibilities, always respecting the autonomy of the subsidiaries and the management responsibility of their governing bodies:

1. approve the FHC's business plan and review its compliance
2. approve the Risk Appetite Framework of the FHC, the policies, the early warning system and the manual of the Risk Management Framework (RMF) and verify compliance
3. decide on the need to take action, and if applicable, follow up on its application and effectiveness, when it is aware of: (i) material variations in exposures to the risks inherent to the FC and deviations from the thresholds and limits of the RMF and (ii) weaknesses in the RMF to perform risk management in accordance with the economies and markets where the FC operates, its level of capital, regulatory framework, business plan, and appetite and risk profile
4. evaluate, at least once a year, the effectiveness of the RMF order to adequately manage the risks and adopt the appropriate measures
5. designate the members of the risk committee and approve its regulations

In the case of FCs, the board of the holding company is responsible for issuing policies in this regard and ensuring that they are complied with throughout the entities of the FC. However, governing bodies of the entities individually considered are still responsible for the supervision of the internal control system in each of them, as well as everything that it incorporates.

In order to implement Law 1870, Circular externa 013 of 2019 requires that FHCs must design, implement and maintain an RMF for managing the risks of the FC (contagion, concentration and strategic). In addition, the RMF lets the FHCs have a general knowledge of the risks of the entities that make up a FC, without prejudice to the responsibility of each of those entities to manage their risks and their own business.

Additionally, there is a second relevant Circular 012 of 2019, which presents instructions related to the appropriate level of capital of the FC.

Thanks to the new law that gives the SFC greater authority to oversee and obtain information from HFC of FCs, the SFC expects to have a clearer spectrum of the performance of those boards of directors and their effectiveness in this specific role over the next years.

Since the new Law of FCs came into effect on 6 February 2019, and its regulatory decrees have only recently come into force, it is too soon to assess its implementation.

Colombian Code of Best Practices of Corporate Governance—Country Code

The Colombian Code of Best Practices of Corporate Governance applies to financial and non-financial securities issuers that operate in the Colombian financial market and establishes the principle of comply or explain. The first edition of this country code was published in 2007.

However, subsequent developments outlined below required revision of the original code:

- the increasing importance of Multilatinas during Colombia's entry into the OECD accession process, which was initiated in 2013
- the need to have a legal framework for complex company groups with subsidiaries abroad

increasing market consciousness about the importance of corporate governance, especially concerning duties of boards of directors[7], audit committees and independent directors in holding and subsidiary companiesIn September 2014, the SFC, with the support of several private business associations, issued Circular externa 028 of 2014, which launched the New Code of Best Corporate Practices—Country Code.

In its formal structure, the new Country Code is similar to its 2007 version. Consequently, it still identifies five major corporate governance areas, and within them, thirty-three concrete measures on key governance aspects. To allow for better understanding and facilitate progress, some measures are divided into numbered recommendations (in total, 148 recommendations).

The Country Code includes recommendations on the dynamics and operation of the board of directors and control architecture, which address remuneration of the members of the board of directors and of the senior managers, risk management and internal control matters.

This new Country Code includes 23 recommendations aimed exclusively at FCs with an implementation level of 74.98% according to the report of 2018. Some of those provisions are:

- Annual corporate governance reports for groups should include a clear and integral view of all the subsidiaries, in order to provide an informed opinion of organisation, complexity, activities, size and the corporate governance model of the group to the public.
- Boards of holding companies should promote a control environment with a consolidated scope that includes all subsidiaries, defining policies and clear reporting lines to have an integrated risk view of the group.
- Risk management should be managed in a consolidated manner.
- For some groups, it is recommended to have a chief risk officer with scope and authority over all subsidiaries.

The new Country Code provides a clearer spectrum than the 2007 edition and recommends the development of several corporate policies to define and disclose governance practices in company groups.

This code takes an overall approach to corporate governance of company groups, recommending that the holding company steer the group, without prejudice to the independence of the subsidiaries, including that:

- The holding company board should have a decision-making process clearly defined, which includes a comprehensive and consolidated vision of the companies that make up the group. The holding company board should have the authority to define the ownership structure, corporate governance model as well as management of conflicts of interests, financial and investment policies of the group.

- The board or executive committees of parent companies should coordinate responsibilities with decision-makers of subsidiaries.
- The subsidiary board may decide not to create board committees to deal with certain matters that may be assumed by the holding company or its board committees. However, this is not intended to imply a transfer of the responsibilities of subordinate boards to the holding company.
- The holding company should require board evaluations for all boards within a group.
- The holding company board should create a "related parties map" in which board members and executives report their relationships that may create conflicts of interests.
- The holding company board should establish a formal Related Party Transactions Policy in which it defines the procedure to evaluate, approve and disclose related party transactions.

Consequently, the new Country Code motivates issuers to delegate the functions of the board in a balanced way, ensuring the fulfilment of all essential and inalienable duties. Among such functions are the so-called general strategic-definition functions, the supervision of key matters and the control of the ordinary course of business and governance.

The board of directors may request the advice or technical support of its specialised committees to perform its functions and to take decisions effectively. The Code has 12 recommendations specifically for boards of FCs or company groups.

In addition, the Country Code establishes as a board function: (R.13.1)

> *"ii. Defining the corporation's structure. In the case of a conglomerate, the Board of Directors of the parent company will define the structure and/or governance model for it.*
>
> *ix. Approving the risk policy, identifying and monitoring periodically the corporation's main risks, including those assumed in off-balance sheet transactions".*

There is no difference in regulatory approach or framework when some or several of the companies are listed or have minority shareholders.

Main elements and rationale for the current regulatory approach

Intra-group transactions, guarantees and commitments

According to current Colombian laws and regulations, there are prohibitions and/or burdens related to the group relationships, namely:

- **Interlocking.** Article 262 of the Commercial Code prohibits subordinated companies from in any manner having an interest, quota or share in the controlling companies (circular ownership). Transactions executed contravening this norm will be void.
- **Verification of the Operations' Existence.** Article 265 of the Commercial Code sets forth that the inspection, surveillance and control bodies may verify the existence of operations executed by the parent or controlling company with its subordinated companies to confirm the existence or non-existence of such operations or their execution under conditions significantly different to market conditions and being damaging to the state, the partners or third parties.

  In any of the above cases, the supervisory body will be able to apply fines and, if considered necessary, request that such operations be suspended. The above applies without prejudice to the actions of the partners and third parties to obtain the corresponding indemnifications.
- **Special Report.** Article 29 of Law 222 of 1995 indicates that, in cases involving a corporate group as defined by the Commercial Code, the management of the controlled companies and of the controlling company must submit a special report each year to the respective Annual General

Meeting (AGM), presenting a summary of the economic relationships between group companies during the previous accounting period.

- **Consolidation of Financial Statements.** Article 35 of Law 222 of 1995 includes the obligation to prepare, submit, and disclose consolidated general-purpose financial statements (Article 23 of Decree 2649 of 1993 and IFRS 10—Consolidated Financial Statements).
- **Conflicts of Interest.** Article 23 of Law 222 of 1995 requires directors and officers in company groups to refrain from participating by themselves or through third parties in activities that represent a permanent conflict of interest with its company, unless expressly authorised by the AGM.
- **Financial Conglomerates**. Regarding FCs, there are thresholds and other rules more specific than the general commercial law.

The role and duties of the board with respect to such transactions, guarantees and commitments is addressed in Article 265 of the Commercial Code and Decree 1486, as described above.

Limitations on Active Credit Operations

Article 122 of the Organic Statute of the Financial System establishes limitations on active credit operations:

- **Operations with partners or administrators and their relatives.** The authorised operations determined by the National Government and held by the entities supervised by the SFC, with their shareholders holding 5% or more of the subscribed capital, with their administrators, as well as those that they celebrate with the spouses and relatives of their partners and administrators within the second degree of consanguinity or affinity, or only civil, will require approval of the unanimous vote of the members of the board of directors attending the respective meeting.

  In the minutes of the corresponding meeting of the board of directors, a record shall be kept of the compliance with the rules on limits to the granting of credit or maximum limits of indebtedness or concentration of risks in force on the date of approval of the operation.

  In these operations, conditions different from those generally used by the entity to the public may not be agreed, depending on the type of operation, except for those that are celebrated with the administrators to meet their health, education, housing and transportation needs in accordance with the regulations that for this purpose previously determined by the board of directors in a general manner.

Transparency, disclosure and the right to Information

Ownership disclosure of companies in the real sector depends on the type of company. Stock companies are in general reluctant to identify shareholders. In quota companies, such as limited liability companies and simple limited partnership companies, the names of the partners should be reported to the mercantile registry.

However, according to Article 30 of Law 222 of 1995, commercial companies must register Control and/or Business Group situations and its amendments in the public commercial register kept by the Chambers of Commerce corresponding to the registered office of the parent company and the subsidiaries.

Current accounting norms include the obligation to make significant disclosures. For instance, IFRS 12 and Section 9 require disclosure of information related to the nature of company participation in other entities, the associated risks and the effects they may have on the controlling persons. Other examples include IFRS3 Business Combinations, IFRS10 Consolidated Financial Statements, IAS 1 Presentation of Financial Statements and IAS 24 Related Party Disclosures.

Regarding ownership and control structure, issuers of securities that are part of a group must disclose[8] to the Registro Nacional de Valores y Emisores (RNVE) the control situation as part of "relevant information".

In addition, any change in the ownership structure of the issuer that exceeds 5% of its subscribed capital must be immediately reported to the market as relevant information through the RNVE.

Financial institutions must file the Form 529 to the SFC, which lays out shareholding structure, detailing holdings above 1% of capital up to the third level of ownership, and Article 53 of the Organic Statute of the Financial System (EOSF) empowers the SFC to require at any time any information on beneficial owners of their capital.

Overall, listed companies and financial institutions must disclose:

- Changes in the issuer's control situation, in accordance with the provisions in Articles 260 and 261 of the Commercial Code, whether the case of exclusive or joint control.
- Changes in shareholder structure, equal to or greater than 5% of the outstanding shares of the company, either directly or indirectly, through natural or legal persons with which a sole beneficial owner is settled.
- Capital investments in domestic or foreign companies involving a subsidiary relationship.

In the case of conglomerates, disclosure of information related to the group of companies to third parties is comprehensive and transversal, which allows outside parties to form an opinion based on reality, organisation, complexity, activities, size and the Conglomerate's governance model. *(Recommendation 30.2 Country Code)*.

Recently, the SFC issued Circular externa 018 of 2018 that regulates the information regarding the share composition reports of entities monitored and/or controlled, shareholders of the first, second, third level and persons who exercise final effective control.[9]

Disclosure of aspects of ownership and control

In addition to share ownership, supervised entities and issuers must reveal the controller, the beneficial owner[10] and the structure by which control is exercised. In the case of issuers of securities, the type of action and whether it confers a vote or not must be disclosed.

In the case of registration and disclosure to the market done through the Chambers of Commerce[11], this includes the controller—who determines the decisions in the company or group of companies—and the entire chain of ownership through which such control is exercised, should it be indirect.

As provided in #12, Lit. b) of Article 5.2.4.1.5 of Decree 2555 of 2010, shareholder agreements must be disclosed immediately as relevant information, once they have been deposited in the registered office of the company[12]. Additionally, if a person exercises control or joint control occurs because of a shareholder agreement or other type of contract, , there is an obligation to register such a situation before the Chamber of Commerce, indicating the ground that settles it.

Rights to information

In general, minority shareholders have the right to access the information held by any other shareholder in the AGM by exercising the right of inspection.

Subsidiaries abroad have confidentiality limits established in the local law regarding access to information, however Colombian authorities have access to public information such as financial information.

Requirements related to treatment of shareholders

Regarding non-financial companies, Article 24 of Law 1564 of 2012 establishes the General Procedural Code and gives the Superintendency of Companies exclusive jurisdictional powers to review the validity of votes at the AGM in case of a shareholder's abusive use of the right to vote (for both listed and non-listed companies).

Specifically, this regulation refers to *"the total annulment of a decision adopted in abuse of the right on the grounds of illicit purpose and compensation for damages in the case of majority, minority and parity abuse when shareholders do not exercise their right to vote in the interest of the company and for the purpose of causing damage to the company or to the other shareholders or of obtaining unjustified advantage for themselves or a third party as well as when the vote may result in damage to the company or the other shareholders."*

In addition, Colombian legislation establishes special mechanisms for the protection of minority shareholders such as those in Article 141 of Law 446 of 1998, under which any group of shareholders that represent less than a 10% participation in a company and are not represented on its board, can request the intervention of the SFC whenever they consider that a decision by the shareholders' meeting, the board or an enterprise's legal representatives is directly or indirectly detrimental to their rights.

Regarding securities issuers, Article 40 of Law 964 of 2005 covers "*protection of shareholders. When a plural number of shareholders representing at least five percent (5%) of the subscribed shares submit proposals to the boards of the registered companies, said bodies must consider them and answer them in writing to those who have made them, indicating clearly the reasons that motivated the decisions".*

Other important norms establish exit rights in the event of a merger, spin-off or transformation and high voting quorums for sensitive matters such as profit distribution (78% quorum); the issue of ordinary shares placed without being subject to preferential rights (70% quorum); and payment of dividends in the form of treasury shares (80% quorum).

Recent case law developments

Regarding non-financial company groups, there are two important instances of case law about company groups:

- **Industrial Hullera S.A.** was a Colombian company dedicated to the extraction of coal. It had as parent three important Colombian companies which held 96.73% of its capital and at the same time bought 99.20% of its production below market prices. Those three companies exercised joint control over Hullera S.A.

  The coal company had many problems caused by the mismanagement of its parent companies and labour liabilities, and went into bankruptcy. The Supreme Court declared the parent companies responsible for the bankruptcy and in addition ordered them to pay all the debts of its subsidiary. Finally, in 2015, the Superintendency of Companies declared the liquidation of the company.
- **Almacenes Éxito S.A.** is the largest retail company in Colombia, and it is a Grupo Exito subsidiary. In July 2015, Almacenes Éxito (AE) announced its intention to expand its operations regionally through the acquisition of 50% of the shares of GPA in Brazil and 100% of the shares of Libertad in Argentina, using both cash and credit from a consortium of domestic and foreign banks. AE is ultimately controlled by Casino (holder of 55% of shares), a French-based company which also fully controlled GPA Brazil (through an intermediary firm, Ségisor) and Libertad Argentina (through a pyramidal structure).

  AE followed several procedures in accordance with Colombian regulations and good corporate governance practices, particularly with respect to RPTs and the management of conflicts of interest.

First, two external independent advisors were hired to assess the fairness of the transaction; one of them exclusively advised AE, while the other advised both AE and Casino. Second, the nomination, compensation and corporate governance committee acknowledged the transaction as an RPT and analysed the appropriateness, conditions and prices of the transaction to ensure it would be conducted at arm's length. Also, the conflict of interest committee was convened to issue a few recommendations to be followed in the discussion and approval of the proposed transactions, given the evident conflict of interest for some of the board members.

Finally, after receiving the external appraisals and recommendations of both committees, the board met and decided (without the participation of interested board members) to submit the proposal for approval of the transaction to an extraordinary shareholders meeting. The transaction was finally approved by a 66% majority vote of shareholders in August 2015, which included the votes of the controller (Casino) and certain minority shareholders.

Despite following established procedures, a significant portion of minority shareholders openly expressed their refusal to approve the transactions on the grounds that additional information and analysis were needed. Indeed, the market reacted negatively to this transaction, at least in the short-term when the value of the stock dropped more than twice the COLCAP market index between July and August.

A minority shareholder filed a claim against AE for the inefficacy of the decision taken by the shareholders extraordinary meeting[13], because he considered the decision should have been approved by the board of directors rather than by the shareholders meeting. In the first instance the Superintendency of Companies supported the claim of the minority shareholder, but in the second instance the Superior Tribunal of Bogotá granted AE´s appeal and annulled the judgement of the Superintendency.

Principal issues and concerns with respect to corporate governance in company groups

The Financial Superintendency devotes considerable resources to monitoring and reviewing transactions among company groups and FCs. Academic studies of Colombian groups have found that companies affiliated with company groups actually enjoy better market valuation and better performance than non-affiliated entities. However, there are some issues regarding corporate governance in groups that could be considered as concerns, among others:

- The strong presence of company groups with high ownership concentration, combined with use of preference shares and cross-shareholdings or pyramidal structures could increase the differentiation between cash flow and control rights, and may cause risks to the minority shareholder(s). In addition, they may use intra-group transactions to extract private benefits that are not shared with outside investors in the group.
- The low trading volumes and a gradually diminishing number of listed companies on the BVC, as well as concentrated ownership in the context of large conglomerates result in the regulatory and supervisory authorities strongly focusing on tracking ownership structures and related party transactions among companies within these groups. In this regard, authorities must ensure adequate disclosure and to require appropriate treatment of conflicts of interest.
- The expansion of company groups has increased demands on corporate governance systems, including on the composition of boards of directors in subsidiaries, risk management and compliance assurance, the interaction between internal and external audit mechanisms and treatment of foreign minority shareholders.
- Previous situations exposed the need for new regulatory standards to promote, among other things, the strengthening of the supervision of FCs. The Colombian set of FC regulations represent, on the one hand, a strengthening of the surveillance perspective of the SFC, and on the other hand, requires higher standards from the FCs.

Country code

According to the 2018 Implementation Report, some of the recommendations with **lower** levels of implementation among issuers which are partially related to FCs were:

- **Recommendation 22.2.** (52.32%) The company's policy on operations with related parties addresses the following aspects: i. Assessment, ii. Approval, iii. Disclosure. Only two of the four biggest FCs in Colombia adopted this Recommendation.
- **Recommendation 19.9.** (61.90%) On an annual basis, the board of directors evaluates the effectiveness of its work as a collegiate body, as well as the effectiveness of its Committees and individual members, including evaluation by peers. Only two of the four biggest FCs in Colombia adopted this Recommendation.
- **Recommendation 21.4.** (66.67%) Relevant conflicts of interest, understood as those that would force the affected person to refrain from attending a meeting and/or voting, have been included in the public information published on an annual basis by the company on its website. Only three of the four biggest FCs adopted this Recommendation.

Conclusions: Improvements Needed and Corporate Governance Challenges

The Colombian government, regulators and supervisory entities have made efforts to introduce requirements to strengthen the corporate governance of company groups. Law 1870, its decree and the Circulares externas define the scope of the supervision of FCs in Colombia with the purpose of ensuring the stability of the financial system. Among the intervention instruments provided for in the law is to give instructions related to corporate governance, conflicts of interest, disclosure of information and internal control that must be applied by the entities that make up an FC.

The compliance with the new Country Code by company groups has increased considerably year to year. It indicates that companies have seen the positive effects of implementing corporate governance practices in their businesses. The SFC has found higher standards of administration and management, higher levels of transparency, increasing trust on the part of financial consumers and minority shareholders in entities.

Some other important advances seen in companies after implementing corporate governance in company groups are:

- They established support committees for the board to make their work more effective and take the right decisions in a timely manner.
- They defined high standards in control environments in order to get a consolidated vision of risks that gathered all the business of its subordinates.
- They have robust information mechanisms given the complexity of their businesses, which make them be more trusted in the market.

However, there are further implementation efforts that are needed in company groups to improve their corporate governance and the professionalism of all agents:

- strong improvements in the processes of identification, disclosure and administration of conflicts of interest and RPTs
- strengthening the independence and professionalism of the boards of directors and their support committees (e.g. investments, risks, auditing and administration of conflicts of interest)
- adequate board consideration of products and services offered by supervised entities (including governance issues related to advice, transparency, incentive alignment and quality of management vis-à-vis investors)
- a much more effective control architecture

In addition, considering the dynamism and evolution of the market, Colombian governmental entities have some challenges to make company groups implement into their internal corporate governance the following aspects:

- continue advancing in the strengthening of corporate governance, in line with the G20/OECD Principles of Corporate Governance
- achieve greater transparency around the risks associated with the business and its management, including environmental, social and governance factors (ESG)
- educate all market players about the benefits of implementing good corporate governance practices
- innovate in mechanisms of relationships with investors

References

Ministry of Finance and Public Credit of Colombia (2018), Decree 1486 of 6 August, http://es.presidencia.gov.co/normativa/normativa/DECRETO%201486%20DEL%2006%20DE%20AGOSTO%20DE%202018.pdf.

OECD (2015), *G20/OECD Principles of Corporate Governance*, OECD Publishing, Paris, https://doi.org/10.1787/9789264236882-en.

SFC (2019), Corporate Governance Regulations, https://www.superfinanciera.gov.co/inicio/normativa/normativa-gobierno-corporativo-13103.

SFC (2017), Law 1870 of 2017 on supervision and regulation of FCs, https://dapre.presidencia.gov.co/normativa/normativa/LEY%201870%20DEL%2021%20DE%20SEPTIEMBRE%20DE%202017.pdf.

Notes

[1] Law 1870 of 2017 on supervision and regulation of FCs can be found in Spanish on the SFC website.

[2] The Superintendency of Companies regulates and supervises commercial companies, branches of foreign companies, sole proprietorships and any other entities determined by Colombian law. However, if any of those companies are issuers of securities, the supervision is shared with the Financial Superintendency (SFC) whose control function is limited to verifying that issuers adjust their operations to the rules that regulate the stock market and to ensure the timeliness and sufficiency of the information that must be reported to the stock market.

Likewise, the Superintendency of Companies shares the supervision function with the SFC regarding financial holding companies. The first organisation supervises the holding companies, while the SFC supervises them only in relation to the topics established in the law 1870 of 2017 and its regulation (risk management, adequate levels of capital and corporate governance).

In addition, the SFC maintains the objective to supervise the Colombian financial system in order to preserve its stability, security and confidence, as well as to promote, organize and develop the Colombian stock market and the protection of investors, savers and policyholders.

This means that the SFC exercises inspection, surveillance and control over people who carry out financial, stock exchange, insurance and any other activities related to the management, use or investment of resources obtained from the public.

[3] According to the Colombian Commercial register.

[4] Under supervision of the Financial Superintendency of Colombia (SFC)

[5] As of 31 December 2018.

[6] Decree 1486: August 6, 2018 Regulation on related parties, conflicts of interest and limits of exposure and concentration of risks can be found in Spanish on the Colombian government website.

[7] Colombian Country Code Recommendations regarding boards of directors, specifically for FC or company groups can be found on the Superfinanciera website.

[8] Lit. b), # 9 of Article 5.2 .4.1.5 of Decree 2555 of 2010.

[9] The Circular establishes that issuers must disclose their 25 principal direct shareholders, the second and third level shareholders and the final beneficial owner, the latter, regardless of the level where it is located.

[10] According to Colombian legislation, a beneficial owner is understood as any person or group of persons who, directly or indirectly, by contract, agreement or otherwise, has the right or the power to vote in the election of managers or, to lead, guide and control that vote regarding a share.

[11] The Chambers of Commerce are private entities (non-profit organizations) with delegated regulatory functions, according to Law 28 of 1931, such as the maintenance of public registries. The Chambers of Commerce are the authorized entities in Colombia to perform the functions as a Public Mercantile Registry. There are 57 Chambers of Commerce and each of them has a territorial scope. The Superintendency of Industry and Commerce has the attribution to supervise and sanction Chambers of Commerce.

[12] As provided in Article 43 of Law 964 of 2005

[13] In Colombian law **inefficacy** means the decision does **not** produce effects in law, while **nullity**, means that the decision produces effects until an authority annuls the decision.

3 India case study

This chapter on India highlights the long-standing importance of company groups in India's economy and focuses particularly on two major laws that apply to such groups in India: the Companies Act, 2013 applying to all companies, and the Securities and Exchange Board of India (Listing Obligations and Disclosure Requirements) Regulations, 2015, applying to listed entities. The chapter describes the rationale for India's regulatory approach, highlighting important issues and concerns with respect to company groups. These include issues such as disclosure of capital structures and control arrangements; the rights to obtain information about other entities in the group; the framework with respect to related party transactions; and risk management, control systems and group policies.

Introduction

World over, companies exist through group structures—i.e. they are a part of a group of companies that are linked through ownership and/or other mechanisms to exercise control—for a variety of reasons including business, legal and governance.

Such holding-subsidiary relationships are often prevalent because of various advantages that such structures may offer to the companies/group. For instance, such structure may facilitate reduction of risk at the holding company level by exporting the same to subsidiaries. Subsidiaries may also facilitate diversification of the business of the corporate group; they can also be in the form of special purpose vehicles for holding companies to enter into acquisitions or joint ventures. Such structures may also enable segregation of different businesses including specific assets and liabilities relating to such business into separate entities and also specific funding into such businesses.

While the group structure may help to fulfil many business objectives as stated above, it is also fraught with certain dangers/concerns. The most common of such concerns pertain to related party transactions arising out of the conflict of interest that is inherent in a group structure. In countries such as India, where there are dominant controlling shareholders (promoters), the concern is exacerbated since such situations lend themselves to an increased possibility of abuse. More serious concerns such as those pertaining to siphoning off of funds, tax evasion, use of such structures to create shell companies, masking of unaccounted funds, etc. may also arise in several group structures.

Therefore, regulators around the world have put in place various filters to address these concerns and ensure robust group governance.

In India, the concept of group structures is as old as company law itself, which runs more than a hundred years. Companies exist through groups and there are different purposes for which group companies are formed. The very issues that have plagued group structures around the world have found their examples in the Indian context too; this has led to the regulators enacting law to facilitate groups while keeping a check on the negatives.

This case study is primarily based on two major laws that apply to company groups in India—the Companies Act, 2013 and the Securities and Exchange Board of India (Listing Obligations and Disclosure Requirements) Regulations, 2015 (SEBI LODR Regulations). While the former applies to all companies, the latter applies to listed entities in particular.

This chapter attempts to explain various concerns in India regarding company groups and the requirements which have been put in place to address these concerns. An attempt has been made to explain the regulatory requirements in a simplified manner in the five sections in the case study, with detailed technical provisions referenced through notes providing web links to the legal texts at the end of this chapter.

Context, background and national discussion

Prevalence of group structures in India

The most prevalent form of group structures in India is through holding company-subsidiary relationships. A figurative explanation of a simplified company group structure is given below for reference.

Figure 3.1. Explanation of a simplified company group structure

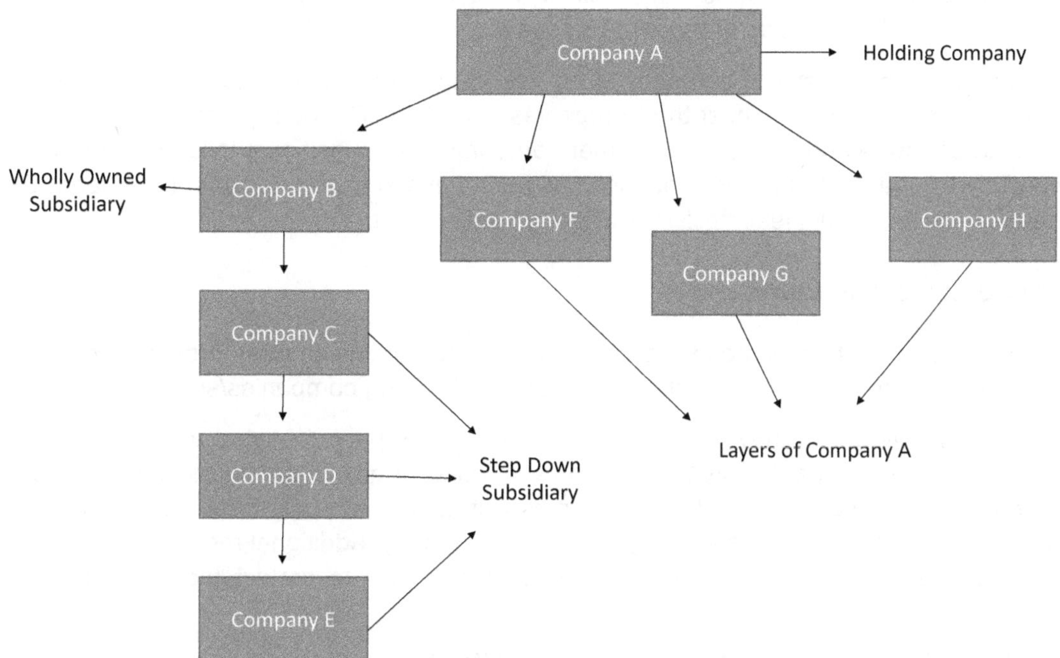

Several of such companies at different layers may become 'associates' of each other since they belong to the same group.

Accordingly, many unlisted and listed entities[1] in India are part of group structures. These structures may be created for different purposes that may be functional, financial, administrative, legal, etc.

A preliminary study of the top 500 listed entities in India by market capitalisation[2] indicates the following:

1. Every listed entity in the top 500 by market capitalisation has at least one subsidiary (*including step-down subsidiaries in several cases*) or a holding company or an associate[3].
2. On a simple average and median basis, a listed entity has around 18 and six subsidiaries /associates/holding company in totality respectively.
3. 20 listed entities among the top 500 have 100 or more subsidiaries /associates /holding companies in totality, the highest being company with 308 subsidiaries/associates/holding company. These may be considered as entities belonging to large groups.
4. On the other hand, it may also be noted that 297 entities (*~2/3rd of the total number of entities*) have less than ten subsidiaries/associates/holding companies in totality.

Several countries have cross-shareholdings as a major form of group structure. However, in India, the pyramid structure, mainly revolving around holding company-subsidiary relationships, is the most common construct of company group structures as can be seen from the data above.

Definition of 'company groups'

While the term *'company group' per se* is not defined in company law/accounting law/securities law in India, the terms *group company[4]', 'holding company[5]', 'subsidiary[6]' and 'associate company[7]* have been defined under the Companies Act, 2013[8]/SEBI Regulations/Indian Accounting Standards.

The following two main criteria have been laid down under the Companies Act, 2013 for determining whether a company is a subsidiary of another company:

1. control over the composition of the board of directors of such company
2. exercise/control over more than one-half of the total share capital of such company *(whether directly or together with one or more of its subsidiary companies)*

For the determination of whether a company is an associate company of another company, the test of *'significant influence'* is laid down under the Companies Act, 2013. Therefore, a company is considered to be an associate of another company if such other company has a significant influence in it (*but which is not its subsidiary company*). Significant influence has been defined to means control of at least **20** percent of total share capital, or of business decisions under an agreement.

Legal requirements and concerns

While the legal requirements have been detailed in section two of this chapter, broadly, India has several legal/regulatory requirements with respect to group entities (holding companies/subsidiaries/associates).

Quite a few legal requirements have been laid down for all companies—listed and unlisted, public and private—under the Companies Act, 2013. Therefore, in case of group structures, which constitute only unlisted companies, the provisions of the Companies Act, 2013 will apply to all such companies in the group. However, if any of the entities in the group is a listed entity, additional requirements are laid down in SEBI Regulations with respect to such structures with a view to protect the interest of the public investors.

In case of listed entities, the requirements significantly differ if the listed entity itself is a holding company *vis-à-vis* a structure whether the listed entity is a subsidiary of another company as explained in detail in section two of this chapter.

The legal requirements and issues of concern differ depending on the characteristics of the group. The legal/regulatory requirements with respect to a holding company-subsidiary relationship are generally much higher compared to that with/between associates.

While the concerns regarding complex group structures have been detailed in section two, broadly, the concerns on group structures in India are largely similar to the concerns globally on such structures such as lack of transparency, potential abuse of related party transactions, etc.

Main elements and rationale for the current regulatory approach

Regulatory requirements—Overview

The Companies Act, 2013 and SEBI Regulations address specific situations in the company group context, broadly:

1. requirements with respect to all companies under the Companies Act, 2013
2. additional requirements if one or more listed entity/entities is part of the group *(under SEBI Regulations):*
    a. requirements if the listed entity is the holding company and has subsidiaries
    b. requirements if the listed entity itself is a subsidiary (i.e. it has a holding company/where another company is its 'promoter' *(it may be noted that the term 'promoter'*[9] *may be largely unique to India)*

Specific regulatory requirements

The specific regulatory requirements as per the aforesaid classification are as under:

- Legal requirements for all companies under Companies Act, 2013:

The legal requirements with respect to subsidiaries, associates and holding companies in Companies Act are given below:

1. Restriction on the number of layers of subsidiaries[10]: Accordingly, no company shall have more than two layers of subsidiaries, excluding one layer of wholly owned (100%) subsidiaries.
2. Subsidiary company not to hold shares in its holding company.[11] No company shall, either by itself or through its nominees, hold any shares in its holding company and no holding company shall allot or transfer its shares to any of its subsidiary companies and any such allotment or transfer of shares of a company to its subsidiary company shall be void (subject to certain conditions).
3. Mandatory annual consolidation of accounts and disclosure of subsidiary accounts[12]: Where a company has one or more subsidiaries, in addition to annual standalone financial statements, it is required to prepare a consolidated financial statement of the company and of all the subsidiaries (*listed/unlisted*) in the same form and manner as that of its own. Such financial statements are required to be presented to the annual general meeting of the company along with the presentation of its financial statements. (*It may be noted that listed entities are mandatorily required to submit consolidated accounts on a quarterly basis under SEBI Regulations.*)
4. Disclosure of subsidiary accounts[13]: Every company having a subsidiary or subsidiaries is required to:
   - place separate audited accounts in respect to each of its subsidiary on its website, if any;
   - provide a copy of separate audited financial statements in respect to each of its subsidiaries, to any shareholder of the company who asks for it. Further, a company is required to, along with its financial statements to be filed with the Registrar, attach the accounts of its subsidiary or subsidiaries that have been incorporated outside India and which have not established their place of business in India.
5. Disclosures pertaining to subsidiaries, holding companies and associates in the Annual report on shareholding, current investments, dividends, provisions for losses etc.[14] and disclosure of various particulars of subsidiary companies in the annual return submitted to the Registrar of Companies[15]
6. Provisions pertaining to merger and amalgamation of companies, including between a holding company and its wholly owned subsidiary.[16]
7. Conditions with respect to related party transactions such as consent of the Board of Directors, shareholder's approval (majority of minority), disclosures, etc. apply to transactions of the company with its holding company/ subsidiary/ associate companies (if not in ordinary course of business or not at arm's length). However, shareholders' approval is not required for transactions entered into between a holding company and its wholly owned subsidiary whose accounts are consolidated with such holding company and placed before the shareholders at the general meeting for approval. The detailed framework for related party transactions is given in section 4.
8. Employee Stock Options may be provided to the directors, officers or employees of a company's holding company or its subsidiary[17].
9. Restrictions on buyback of own shares through subsidiaries[18].
10. Restriction on investment through more than two layers of investment companies: A company, unless otherwise prescribed, is not permitted to make investment through more than two layers of investment companies. However, certain exemptions are given in this respect[19].
11. Conditions for determining the independence of a director for appointment on the Board of Directors of a company as an Independent Director includes checks on relationship/ interest of such director with respect to holding, subsidiary or associate company as well[20].
12. Debar on appointment of auditor associated with holding/ subsidiary/ associate companies[21], right of access to records of subsidiaries is given to auditors[22] and restrictions are placed on auditors of a company providing non-audit services to its holding / subsidiary company[23].

13. Restriction on non-cash transactions with directors is also applicable to directors of holding/ subsidiary/ associate companies[24].
14. Every company is required to keep at its registered office, a register containing such particulars of its directors and key managerial personnel as may be prescribed, which shall include the details of securities held by each of them in the company or its holding, subsidiary, subsidiary of company's holding company or associate companies[25].

These generally apply to all companies—unlisted and listed. Nevertheless, some of the provisions may apply only to a certain set of companies e.g. companies exceeding a certain size.

- Additional legal requirements with respect to listed entities where the listed entity is a holding company:

If a listed entity has a subsidiary/subsidiaries, apart from the requirements under the Companies Act, 2013, additional requirements are specified for listed entities under the SEBI LODR Regulations. The detailed requirements under the SEBI LODR Regulations are given below:

1. Concept of material subsidiaries (whose income or net worth exceeds 10% of the consolidated income or net worth respectively).[26]
2. Mandatory consolidation of accounts on a quarterly basis (with effect from 1 April 2019) In this respect, the statutory auditor of a listed entity is required to undertake a limited review of the audit of all the entities/ companies whose accounts are to be consolidated with the listed entity. Further, the listed entity is required to disclose the effect on the financial results of material changes in the composition of the listed entity, if any, including but not limited to business combinations, acquisitions or disposal of subsidiaries and long term investments, any other form of restructuring and discontinuance of operations.[27]
3. Criteria for determining independence of an independent director includes a check on whether such director/ his relatives is related to the holding/ subsidiary/ associate company including pecuniary relationships, key managerial positions etc.[28]
4. Stricter norms for related party transactions vis-à-vis the requirements under Companies Act, 2013 such as related parties (whether or not they are related to that particular transaction) not being permitted to vote to approve when material transactions are put to vote to shareholders, increased disclosures etc. The detailed framework for related party transactions is given in section 4.
5. Detailed obligations on the listed entity, its board of directors and audit committee with respect to the subsidiaries and certain powers given to the shareholders of the listed entity, including, inter-alia, the following[29]:
    - An independent director on the board of the listed entity to be appointed on the board of material unlisted subsidiaries (Specifically for this provision, the threshold for material subsidiary is considered as 20%).
    - Obligation on the audit committee to review financial statements of unlisted subsidiaries (especially investments made by subsidiaries) and to review utilisation of loans to/advances to/investments in the subsidiaries exceeding a certain threshold.
    - Obligation on the board of directors of the listed entity with respect to minutes of board meetings of the unlisted subsidiaries, significant transactions & arrangements by the unlisted subsidiaries, sale of subsidiaries which are material and not in normal course of business.
    - Restriction on disposal of shares in material subsidiaries.
    - Restrictions on sale/disposal/leasing of material assets of a material subsidiary.
    - Provisions to apply to listed subsidiaries which are itself holding companies in respect to their subsidiaries.

  - Secretarial audit for material unlisted subsidiaries along with that of the listed entity by a practicing company secretary.
  - Group governance unit/Committee/policy (discretionary requirement).[30]
  - Listed entity to disclose separate audited financial statements of each subsidiary on its website in respect of a relevant financial year, uploaded at least 21 days prior to the date of the annual general meeting which has been called to inter-alia consider accounts of that financial year.
  - Disclosure of all events or information with respect to a subsidiary, which are material for the listed entity. In this regard, sale or disposal of any subsidiary of the listed entity is deemed to be a material event, requiring disclosure to the stock exchanges.
  - Disclosure in the annual report of the listed entity, of the total fees for all services paid by the listed entity and its subsidiaries, on a consolidated basis, to the statutory auditor and all entities in the network firm/network entity of which the statutory auditor is a part.
  - Detailed norms with respect to schemes of arrangement where one or more of the entities are listed entities (not applicable for merger of a wholly owned subsidiary with its holding company subject to filing of the schemes with the stock exchanges).
- Legal requirements with respect to listed entities where listed entity is itself a subsidiary/ has a parent company/ promoter:

In India, most of the listed entities have '*promoters*'. The term *'promoters'* in India is generally used to denote those persons instrumental to the time of formation of the company and those who are in control of the company, through shareholding and/or management or otherwise. Therefore, a company who is in control of a listed entity (*including a holding company having control over the listed entity*) is termed as a *'promoter'* of that entity.

Several SEBI Regulations impose obligations on the promoters as well as on the listed entities with respect to such promoters.

Some of the major obligations/requirements on the listed entity with respect to promoters are as under:

1. Related party transactions: In case of transactions with promoters who are related parties, stringent norms such as approval from the audit committee, approval from shareholders (*for material transactions where related parties*[31] *are not permitted to vote to approve the resolution*), disclosures, etc. apply.
2. Disclosures on transactions with certain promoters: The annual report of a listed entity is required to include disclosures of transactions of the listed entity with any person or entity belonging to the promoter/promoter group which hold(s) 10% or more shareholding in the listed entity.
3. Independence criteria: The listed entity must ensure a certain minimum number of independent directors on its board of directors. One of the tenets of independence is that they should not be related to the promoters of such listed entity/its holding company.
4. Disclosure of shareholding of promoters/promoter group: All entities falling under promoter and promoter group are required to be disclosed separately in the shareholding pattern submitted by the listed entities to the stock exchanges.
5. Conditions for re-classification: A listed entity is permitted to re-classify a promoter/person belonging to promoter group as a public shareholder only on satisfaction of certain conditions.
6. Disclosures of promoter related material events: Certain events such as fraud/defaults by promoter are deemed to be material events and are required to be disclosed by the listed entity to the stock exchanges as soon as possible but no later than 24 hours of occurrence of the event.
7. Restriction on remuneration to promoter executive directors: The fees or compensation payable to executive directors who are promoters or members of the promoter group, are subject to the approval of the shareholders by special resolution in general meeting, if (i) the annual remuneration

payable to such executive director exceeds INR 50 million or 2.5% of the net profits of the listed entity, whichever is higher; or (ii) where there is more than one such director, the aggregate annual remuneration to such directors exceeds 5% of the net profits of the listed entity.

Some major obligations/restrictions on promoters with respect to a listed entity are as under:

1. A certain minimum contribution required from promoters in case of a public issue and lock-in provision on such contribution to ensure *'skin-in-the-game'*.
2. Restrictions on preferential allotment of securities to promoters.
3. Detailed disclosure obligations on the promoters with respect to changes in their shareholding, change in control, etc., especially keeping in mind requirements under SEBI's Takeover and the Prohibition of Insider Trading Regulations.
4. Restrictions/conditions imposed with respect to sale of shares by promoters if such persons are *'insiders'* as per the Prohibition of Insider Trading Regulations.
5. Contravention of SEBI Regulations, circulars, etc. may invite freezing of shareholding of promoters/promoter group entities.

Monitoring of financial conglomerates

The importance of addressing systemic risk and supervising Financial Conglomerates came to the forefront subsequent to the 2008 global financial crisis. Monitoring of Financial Conglomerates (FC) got a renewed focus in India with the establishment of the sub-group of Inter Regulatory Forum, under the aegis of FSDC (*Financial Stability and Development Council*) Sub Committee. Financial conglomerate supervision involves assessment of systemic risk posed by a FC group; the focus here being inter-connectedness of group entities and inter-linkages in the financial system.

An FC is defined "on the basis of its significant presence in two or more market segments out of 5 segments (namely, Banking, Insurance, Capital Market, Non-Banking Finance and Pension Fund)". Based on the criteria for identifying financial conglomerates, certain groups have been identified as FCs in India with different regulators acting as the Principal regulators for different FCs depending on the major segments of business.

One of the key processes of existing FC monitoring mechanism includes holding discussions with the executives of the identified FC Group on a regular intervals. These discussions with FC group executives provide the opportunity to understand the Group's focus & business strategy as well as to discuss issues like conglomerates' risk management strategies, system of monitoring of intra-group transactions and exposures, among others and also communicate supervisory concerns, if any.

Rationale for regulatory approach—Important issues and concerns with respect to company groups

As stated earlier, group structures around the world, while having several benefits to various stakeholders, may also give rise to several areas of concern. Many of the issues that have plagued group structures around the world have examples in the Indian context too.

Accordingly, many issues and concerns have been debated and discussed in detail in India in the context of company groups which form the broad foundation for the specific legal requirements with respect to company groups as stated above.

A major concern in complex group structures is the lack of transparency and opaqueness in approach, governance, finances, strategy, etc. The Kotak Committee on corporate governance, in its report to SEBI dated 5 October 2017[32] made detailed recommendations to SEBI on enhanced monitoring of group entities and improvement in group governance. The broad rationale of the Committee on these recommendations is reproduced below:

"As companies grow in scale and operations go global, businesses become more complex. Business and structural compulsions (both legal and financial) often necessitate the creation of holding and operating entities. The Committee notes that several listed entities in India operate through a network of entities-- where some companies have over 200 subsidiaries, step-down subsidiaries, associates, and joint ventures. While investors hold direct equity only in the listed holding company, they have valued the entire business structure at the time of investment. Therefore, it is important for boards to ensure that good governance trickles down to the entire structure. Accordingly, to provide for better transparency on the governance levels of downstream investee entities of the listed entity and to improve the monitoring of the listed entity at a consolidated level, the following recommendations have been made by the Committee…."

Such complexities and opaqueness often present an opportunity to camouflage the actual financials, usage of funds, flow of funds, intra-group transactions, leverage, etc. across the group which may get submerged in the myriad of information that such structures often present. Such opaqueness and complexity in information affect not just the shareholders but a large number of stakeholders including lenders and even the regulators/tax department/government. It is also possible that some of the groups may use such complex structuring for potential diversion of funds, avoidance of tax, concealment of actual leverage, etc.

Another concern that such group structures often generate a potential abuse of related party transactions, especially by the controlling/dominant shareholders to the detriment of the minority shareholders. Similar concerns also exist in India, which are exacerbated by the existence of a large number of promoter-led companies in India. Hence, it may be observed that regulatory requirements with respect to related party transactions are very stringent in India, especially in comparison to global requirements.

Disclosure and the right to information

As is in most of the countries in the world, India has a disclosure based regulation. A disclosure based approach to regulation needs to be dynamic and evolutionary since the essence is in the disclosure. Therefore, SEBI has been continuously focusing its efforts to build robust disclosure practices by trying to have a dynamic approach to regulation. The Ministry of Corporate Affairs has also, on its part, made a giant stride with the new Companies Act, 2013. These efforts have contributed to India being ranked 7th in the world on the parameter *'Protecting Minority Investors'*[33]as per the latest rankings of World Bank with respect to 'Ease of Doing Business'.

Disclosure of capital structures and control arrangements of the company

Capital structures and control arrangements and changes thereon are reflected from the disclosures relating to financial results and shareholding patterns filed by companies periodically.

Disclosure of capital structures and control arrangements provide two major sources of information relevant to company group structures:

1. **Disclosures of shareholding pattern** of a company gives an insight into the holding structure of that company thereby providing a bird's eye view of companies in the group **which are in control of the concerned company** in the group structure.
2. **Disclosures of investments/assets** of a company gives an insight into the holding by the company into subsidiaries/layers of subsidiaries in the group **which are controlled by the concerned company** in the group structure.

Accordingly, the regulatory requirements in India with respect to disclosure of shareholding and control arrangements of a company largely focus on disclosures on both the above areas. Details of the same are given hereunder:

1. Disclosure of shareholding pattern:
   a. Disclosure of shareholding pattern of a company is required both under Companies Act, 2013 *(applicable to all companies)* and SEBI (Listing Obligations and Disclosure Requirements) Regulations, 2015 *(applicable to listed entities).*
   b. Such disclosures, *inter-alia*, include the following:

As per Companies Act, 2013, in the annual return[34]

   i. Category-wise shareholding e.g. promoters (Indian / foreign), public shareholders (institutions / non-institutions), etc.
   ii. Detailed requirements with respect to shareholding of promoters including names of the promoters, shareholding, shares pledged/encumbered, change in promotor shareholding (shareholding at the beginning and end of the year, date-wise increase / decrease specifying reasons), etc.
   iii. Details of top ten shareholders.
   iv. Shareholding of directors and key management personnel

As per Companies Act, 2013, in financial statements[35]:

   v. For each class of share capital, the following is required to be disclosed:
      - shares in respect of each class in the company held by its holding company or its ultimate holding company including shares held by or by subsidiaries or associates of the holding company or the ultimate holding company in aggregate
      - shares in the company held by each shareholder holding more than 5% shares specifying the number of shares held

As per SEBI LODR Regulations, on a quarterly basis[36]:

   vi. A summary statement of shareholding, including:
      - Category-wise breakup (promoter & promoter group, public shareholders)
      - Fully-paid up, partly paid up shares
      - Number of Voting Rights held in each class of securities
      - Number of Shares pledged or otherwise encumbered
      - Number of Locked in shares
   vii. Detailed disclosures on shareholding of promoter and promoter group
   viii. Detailed disclosures on shareholding of public shareholders including break-up of holding by institutions, government and non-institutions *(Names of the shareholders holding 1% or more than 1% of shares of listed entity are to be disclosed in public category)*

   c. In addition to the immediate shareholders of the company, as stated above, Companies Act, 2013[37] and SEBI LODR Regulations also require disclosure of details of significant beneficial owners *(holding directly or indirectly at least 10% of the shares*) of the company.
   d. In addition to the above, SEBI Takeover Regulations also require regular disclosures, from time to time, if a person/persons acting in concert acquire(s) shares or voting rights in a company beyond a certain threshold. These Regulations also require detailed disclosures to be made with respect to pledge / encumbrance of the shares of promoters.

2. Disclosure of subsidiaries/associates/joint ventures:

a. Under annual disclosures by a company required as per the Companies Act, 2013[38]:

   i. Disclosures in the balance sheet under 'Investments' need to specifically include names of the subsidiaries (*including step-down subsidiaries*) in which investments have been made and the nature and extent of the investment so made.

   ii. Disclosures in the consolidated financial statements also include detailed disclosures on the share of the subsidiaries, associates and joint ventures in the consolidated net assets, profit and loss, etc. This ensures disclosures pertaining to not only the subsidiaries of the company but also its associates and joint ventures.

   iii. A company is also required to additionally disclose a list of subsidiaries or associates or joint ventures which have not been consolidated in the consolidated financial statements along with the reasons for not consolidating.

b. Additionally, SEBI has recently mandated listed entities to submit consolidated results every quarter, which ensures an overall picture of the listed entity and its subsidiaries taken together.

Facets of control other than shareholding

While the disclosures pertaining to shareholding of the company as specified above address one facet of control of the company, holding companies/promoters may also exercise control through other facets. Therefore, disclosure of such other facets are also equally important for a stakeholder to understand the details of the entities who exercise control over the company through non-shareholding facets.

Two major such facets of control are through differential voting rights and shareholder agreements. There are regulatory requirements pertaining to the same in India which are detailed hereunder:

1. Disclosure of voting rights

While Companies Act, 2013 permits a company to have share capital with differential rights as to dividend, voting or otherwise, it is subject to certain conditions. With respect to disclosures of such structures, disclosure of shareholding pattern of a company needs to be separate for each class of shares *(including those with differential voting rights)*.

It may be noted that while dual class shares are permitted to be issued in India (subject to certain conditions), the same is not yet prevalent in India and only a handful of companies have adopted the same. With respect to the listed entities and entities intending to list, SEBI has recently issued a framework for issuance of superior voting rights shares (SR shares); the key provisions are as given below:

a. Eligibility: A company having SR shares is permitted to do an initial public offering (IPO) of only ordinary shares to be listed on the Main Board, subject to fulfilment of eligibility requirements of the SEBI (Issue of Capital and Disclosure Requirements) Regulations, 2018 (SEBI ICDR Regulations) and the following conditions:

   - The issuer company is a tech company i.e. intensive in the use of technology, information technology, intellectual property, data analytics, bio-technology or nano-technology to provide products, services or business platforms with substantial value addition.
   - The SR shareholder should not be a part of the promoter group whose collective net worth exceeds INR 5 billion. While determining the collective net worth, the investment of SR shareholders in the shares of the issuer company shall not be considered.
   - The SR shares have been issued only to the promoters/ founders who hold an executive position in the company.
   - The issue of these SR shares has been authorized by a special resolution passed at a general meeting of the shareholders.

- SR shares have been held for a period of at least 6 months prior to the filing of Red Herring Prospectus (RHP).
- SR shares have voting rights in the ratio of minimum 2:1 to maximum 10:1 compared to ordinary shares.

b. Listing and Lock-in: SR shares shall also be listed on Stock Exchanges after the issuer company makes a public issue. However, SR shares shall be under lock-in after the IPO until their conversion to ordinary shares. Transfer of SR shares among promoters is not permitted. No pledge/ lien is allowed on SR shares.

c. Rights of SR shares: SR shares shall be treated at par with the ordinary equity shares in every respect, including dividends, except in the case of voting on resolutions. The total voting rights of SR shareholders (including ordinary shares), post listing, shall not exceed 74%.

d. Enhanced corporate governance: Companies having SR shareholders shall be subject to enhanced corporate governance as follows:

- At least ½ of the Board and 2/3rd of the Committees (excluding Audit Committee) as prescribed under SEBI LODR Regulations shall comprise of Independent Directors.
- Audit Committee shall comprise of only Independent Directors.

e. Coat-tail Provisions: Post-IPO, the SR Equity Shares shall be treated as ordinary equity shares in terms of voting rights (i.e. one SR share shall have only one vote) in the following circumstances:

- Appointment or removal of independent directors and/or auditor
- In case where promoter is willingly transferring control to another entity
- Related Party Transactions in terms of SEBI LODR Regulations involving SR shareholder
- Voluntary winding up of the company
- Changes in the company's Article of Association or Memorandum - except any changes affecting the SR instrument
- Initiation of a voluntary resolution plan under IBC
- Utilization of funds for purposes other than business
- Substantial value transaction based on materiality threshold as prescribed under LODR
- Passing of special resolution in respect of delisting or buy-back of shares; and
- Any other provisions notified by SEBI in this regard from time to time.

f. Sunset Clauses: SR shares shall be converted into ordinary shares in following circumstances/ events:

- Time Based: The SR shares shall be converted to Ordinary Shares on the 5th anniversary of listing. The validity can be extended once by 5 years through a resolution. SR shareholder would not be permitted to vote on such resolutions.
- Event Based: SR shares shall compulsorily get converted into ordinary shares on occurrence of certain events such as demise, resignation of SR shareholders, merger or acquisition where the control would be no longer with SR shareholder, etc.

g. Fractional Rights Shares: Issue of fractional rights shares by existing listed companies is not allowed. The need for allowing issue of fractional rights shares by listed companies may however be reviewed after gaining enough experience with the use of SR shares.

2. Disclosure of shareholder agreements

Under the SEBI ICDR Regulations, at the time of an IPO, the offer document is required to contain the key terms of all subsisting shareholders' agreements, if any *(to be provided even if the issuer is not a party to such an agreement, but is aware of such an agreement).* Subsequent to listing of the securities, any shareholder agreements (to the extent that it impacts management and control of the listed entity) are required to be disclosed as material events within the timelines as specified. These two requirements ensure disclosures pertaining to shareholder agreements both before and after an IPO.

Additionally, agreements of the promoters/controlling shareholders whereby they pledge their shares to a third party may impact the nature of control such person exercises over the said company. Therefore, disclosures have also been required under the SEBI LODR Regulations and the SEBI Takeover Regulations, with respect to promoters encumbering the shares they hold in the company.

Right to information about other entities in the group

The right of information that various entities in the group *(including promoters/controlling shareholders/subsidiaries)* have with respect to other entities in the group and the overall flow of information between various companies in the group signify the nature and extent of relations between the companies in the group. Therefore, the regulatory requirements surrounding such right to information assumes paramount importance.

Generally, with respect to such right for information, the following are two major types of information that may be sought from a company:

1. information which is already in the public domain (disclosed by the company to the stock exchanges)
2. information which is unpublished and price sensitive.

In the first case, the issue of seeking such information from the company may not arise since the same is already in the public domain.

In the second case, in India, there are several restrictions on seeking of such information from the company under the SEBI (Prohibition of Insider Trading) Regulations, 2015 . The broad requirements in this regard are as under:

1. No insider shall communicate, provide or allow access to any unpublished, price sensitive information, relating to a company or securities listed or proposed to be listed, to any person including other insiders except where such communication is in furtherance of legitimate purposes, performance of duties or discharge of legal obligations.
2. The board of directors of a listed company shall make a policy for determination of *"legitimate purposes"* as a part of "*Codes of Fair Disclosure and Conduct"* formulated under the SEBI (Prohibition of Insider Trading) Regulations.
3. Any person in receipt of unpublished price sensitive information pursuant to a "legitimate purpose" shall be considered an "insider" for purposes of these regulations and due notice shall be given to such persons to maintain confidentiality of such unpublished price sensitive information in compliance with these regulations.
4. The board of directors shall ensure that a structured digital database is maintained containing the names of such persons or entities as the case may be with whom information is shared under this regulation along with the Permanent Account Number or any other identifier authorised by law where Permanent Account Number is not available. Such databases shall be maintained with adequate internal controls and checks such as time stamping and audit trails to ensure non-tampering of the database.

Accordingly, any person (including subsidiaries, shareholders, etc.) may seek unpublished price sensitive information from the company and obtain such information only if it satisfies the conditions as specified above along with other trading restrictions as specified in the Prohibition of Insider Trading Regulations.

Intra-group transactions, guarantees and commitments

While section three provides regulatory requirements with respect to disclosures on control arrangement between various companies in the group, section four attempts to provide details of regulatory requirements with respect to transactions between such companies in the group.

Transactions between various companies in the group, which could be in the nature of sale of goods/services, purchase/lease of property, borrowing relationships, including guarantees, allocation of costs, often provide several advantages to the companies in terms of economies of scale, lower transaction costs, etc. Hence, related party transactions are a normal feature of business in company groups and often have a significant impact on the financial position of the company/group. Notwithstanding these advantages, such transactions also have a significant potential for abuse in view of conflict of interest involved. Hence, regulators across the world have attempted to introduce requirements in order to have a check on such abuse.

In India, a majority of companies continue to be promoter–driven entities with significant shareholding being held by the promoter/promoter group. Therefore, protection of the interests of minority shareholders, especially those of the retail shareholders assumes even more importance. In this context, checks and balances on related party transactions are crucial for good governance of the companies and to prevent abuse by majority shareholders/related parties. Therefore, India has stringent requirements with respect to related party transactions for companies, especially listed entities.

Regulatory provisions with respect to related party transactions in India

Both the Companies Act, 2013[39] and SEBI LODR Regulations[40] have several stringent requirements with respect to related party transactions. A summary of such requirements in placed below:

1. **Approval of the audit committee and the board**: Under SEBI LODR Regulations, all related party transactions by a listed entity require prior approval of the audit committee. Nevertheless, for repetitive transactions, the audit committee is permitted to grant omnibus approval for related party transactions proposed to be entered into by the listed entity subject to certain conditions.
2. After approval of the audit committee, certain transactions are also required to be approved by the board of directors of the company (Companies Act 2013).
3. **Approval of shareholders for material transactions**: In case of material related party transactions, approval of shareholders is required both under Companies Act, 2013 (*for all companies*) and SEBI LODR Regulations (*for listed entities*). Specific thresholds have been laid down under the Companies Act, 2013 and rules specified thereunder and under SEBI LODR Regulations for determination of materiality of the transactions.
4. **Voting by shareholders (majority of minority):** In order to ensure protection of interest of minority shareholders, the Companies Act, 2013 requires that no shareholder shall vote on a resolution, to approve any contract or arrangement which may be entered into by the company, if such member is a related party.
5. SEBI LODR Regulations, applicable to listed entities, have more stringent requirements wherein a related party is not permitted to vote to approve a resolution, whether the entity is a related party to the particular transaction or not.
6. **Disclosure of related party transactions**: Both Companies Act, 2013 and SEBI LODR Regulations have detailed norms with respect to disclosure of related party transactions on an annual basis. Additionally, for listed entities, recently, disclosures on related party transactions have been made mandatory every half-year and on a consolidated basis.

It may be noted that SEBI has on 27 January, 2020, placed for public comments a consultative paper with respect to related party transactions.

Disclosure with respect to guarantees

Under Companies Act, 2013, there are detailed provisions under various Sections[41] which provide for restrictions, disclosures, approval and other requirements with respect to a guarantee given by a company. Such disclosures and other requirements with respect to guarantees are applicable to any guarantee/surety provided by the company to any person, irrespective of whether or not the person is part of the company group. Nevertheless, if the same is a related party transaction, the aforesaid provisions on related party transactions shall apply.

Disclosures of guarantees primarily form a part of the contingent liabilities in the balance sheet of the company. Further, it may also be noted that in general, the accounting standards with respect to off-balance sheet items have been strengthened under the new Ind-AS accounting standards modelled on the lines of IFRS adopted globally.

Under SEBI LODR Regulations, giving of guarantees or indemnity or becoming a surety for any third party is required to be disclosed by a listed entity as a material event *(to be disclosed as soon as possible, not exceeding 24 hours from the date of occurrence of the event)* if the same is material as per the materiality policy of the entity.

It may be noted that SEBI has on 6 March, 2020, placed for public comments, a consultative paper with respect to guarantees provided by a listed entity.

Implementation and monitoring of risk management, control systems and group policies

In general, the board of directors of a company is expected to ensure that appropriate systems of control are in place, in particular, systems for risk management, financial and operational control as far as that specific company is concerned. However, in a group structure, countries differ on obligations of the board of directors of the company as far as overseeing, monitoring and evaluating the implementation of existing risk management systems and compliance with law and relevant standards within the group (*especially its subsidiaries*) are concerned.

In India, certain basic obligations have been laid down on the board of directors of a company under Companies Act, 2013 as far as development and implementation of a risk management policy for the company is concerned including identification therein of elements of risk, if any, which in the opinion of the board may threaten the existence of the company. Further, under the Companies Act, 2013, an obligation has been imposed on the audit committee to evaluate the internal financial controls and risk management systems.

Under SEBI LODR Regulations *(applicable to listed entities)*, there are certain general obligations on the board of directors (*including board committees*) with respect to risk management and control as well as specific obligations with respect to subsidiaries:

1. General obligations on the board of directors (*including board committees*) with respect to risk management and control:
   a. The functions of board of directors including reviewing and guiding of risk policy and ensuring the integrity of the listed entity's accounting and financial reporting systems, including the independent audit, and that appropriate systems of control are in place, in particular, systems for risk management, financial and operational control, and compliance with the law and relevant standards.
   b. The listed entity is required to lay down procedures to inform members of board of directors about risk assessment and minimisation procedures.

c. The board of directors is responsible for framing, implementing and monitoring the risk management plan for the listed entity.

d. The role of the audit committee includes evaluation of internal financial controls and risk management systems.

e. The board of directors of the top 500 listed entities (based on market capitalisation) are required to constitute a Risk Management Committee. The board of directors is required to define the role and responsibility of the Risk Management Committee and may delegate monitoring and reviewing of the risk management plan to the committee and such other functions as it may deem (including cyber security).

2. Specific obligations on the board of directors (*including board committees*) with respect to subsidiaries, especially with respect to risk management and control:

   Certain specific obligations with respect to subsidiaries have been specified in SEBI LODR Regulations *(primarily Regulation 24)* as under:

a. At least one independent director on the board of directors of the listed entity is required to be a director on the board of directors of an unlisted material subsidiary *(income/net worth exceeding 20% of the consolidated value*).

b. The audit committee of the listed entity is required to review the financial statements, in particular, the investments made by the unlisted subsidiary.

c. The minutes of the meetings of the board of directors of the unlisted subsidiary is required to be placed at the meeting of the board of directors of the listed entity.

d. The management of the unlisted subsidiary is required to periodically bring to the notice of the board of directors of the listed entity, a statement of all significant transactions and arrangements (*exceeding 10% of total revenues/expenses/assets/liabilities of the unlisted subsidiary*) entered into by the unlisted subsidiary.

e. Where a listed entity has a listed subsidiary, which is itself a holding company, the aforesaid provisions apply to the listed subsidiary in so far as its subsidiaries are concerned.

f. The audit committee is required to review the utilisation of loans and/or advances from/investment by the holding company in the subsidiary exceeding INR 1 billion or 10% of the asset size of the subsidiary, whichever is lower.

Additionally, where the listed entity has a large number of unlisted subsidiaries, SEBI has issued a circular stating that:

a. The listed entity may monitor their governance through a dedicated group governance unit or Governance Committee comprising the members of its board of directors.

b. A strong and effective group governance policy may be established by the entity.

c. The decision of setting up of such a unit/committee or having such a policy shall lie with the board of directors of the listed entity.

However, it may be noted that the aforesaid requirement of group governance unit/committee/policy is not mandatory on the listed entity. It is the discretion of the listed entity as to whether or not to have such a unit/committee/policy.

Conclusion

The Indian Government and regulators have, over the years, acknowledged various concerns with respect to group structures and have actively introduced various requirements in order to strengthen the governance at the group level. The cap on the maximum number of subsidiaries has been a landmark step in this direction. The requirements prescribed by SEBI with respect to related party transactions by listed entities are one of the most stringent in the world.

Various recent steps of SEBI and the Government also show the focus of India in this direction. For instance, keeping in mind the realities and concerns with respect to information sharing within the group, requirements with respect to information sharing have recently been issued by SEBI under its Insider Trading Regulations. In case a listed entity has many subsidiaries, SEBI has also laid down that the entity may, at its discretion, form a group governance/unit/policy for improving group governance. Other recent initiatives such as strengthening of related party definition and disclosures, mandatory consolidated quarterly financial results, enhanced role of the audit committee to review utilisation of loans/advances/investments to subsidiaries, etc. are also measures which go to exemplify the emphasis on group governance.

Nevertheless, capital markets and the business environment are very dynamic, and robust disclosure, monitoring and enforcement regimes need to evolve to contribute positively to the transparency and efficiency of the corporate framework. India has, particularly during the past few years, zealously pursued such a regime so as to ensure clean disclosures and improved governance so that they add value to all stakeholders. The only way is forward.

References

Ministry of Corporate Affairs of India (2013), India Companies Act 2013, http://ebook.mca.gov.in/default.aspx.

OECD (2015), *G20/OECD Principles of Corporate Governance*, OECD Publishing, Paris, https://doi.org/10.1787/9789264236882-en.

SEBI (2019), List of all SEBI regulations, https://www.sebi.gov.in/sebiweb/home/HomeAction.do?doListing=yes&sid=1&ssid=3&smid=0.

SEBI (2018), Circular of 10 May, https://www.sebi.gov.in/legal/circulars/may-2018/circular-for-implementation-of-certain-recommendations-of-the-committee-on-corporate-governance-under-the-chairmanship-of-shri-uday-kotak_38905.html

SEBI (2017), Report of the committee on corporate governance, https://www.sebi.gov.in/reports/reports/oct-2017/report-of-the-committee-on-corporate-governance_36177.html

World Bank (2019), World Bank Doing Business Database on India, http://www.doingbusiness.org/en/data/exploreeconomies/india

Notes

[1] The term 'listed entities' is used in SEBI (Listing Obligations and Disclosure Requirements) Regulations, 2015 to refer to all entities, in whatever legal form (company or otherwise), which are listed on a recognised stock exchange.

[2] Based on the data provided by National Stock Exchange based on the latest available submissions by these entities.

[3] Based on the annual reports submitted to the National Stock Exchange and the annual returns filed under the Companies Act, 2013.

[4] Refer to regulation 2 (1) (t) of SEBI (Issue of Capital and Disclosure Requirements) Regulations, 2018 for the definition of 'group company', available at the following link:
https://www.sebi.gov.in/legal/regulations/jan-2020/securities-and-exchange-board-of-india-issue-of-capital-and-disclosure-requirements-regulations-2018-last-amended-on-january-01-2020-_41542.html.

[5] Refer to section 2 (46) of Companies Act, 2013 for the definition of 'holding company', available at the following link: http://ebook.mca.gov.in/default.aspx.

[6] Refer to section 2 (87) of Companies Act, 2013 for the definition of 'subsidiary / subsidiary company'. The concept of a subsidiary is also significant from the point of view of presentation of financial statements. The Indian Accounting Standard 27 (IAS 27), which is also converged with the IFRS, specifies that the financial statements of a group in which the assets, liabilities, equity, income, expenses and cash flows of the parent and its subsidiaries are presented as those of a single economic entity are consolidated financial statements. The IAS 110, which deals with consolidated financial statements, states that:
An investor (read 'holding company') controls an investee (read 'subsidiary company') if and only if the investor has all the following:
(a) power over the investee;
(b) exposure, or rights, to variable returns from its involvement with the investee; and
(c) the ability to use its power over the investee to affect the amount of the investor's returns.
The IAS 110 also states that an investor that holds more than half of the voting rights of an investee has power over the investee.
[7] Refer to section 2 (6) of Companies Act, 2013 for the definition of 'associate company'.

[8] The company law in India was governed by the Companies Act, 1956 for more than 50 years, till it was replaced, recently in 2013, by the Companies Act, 2013. So, though most of the companies that exist today in India, including their subsidiaries, have been incorporated under the provisions of the Companies Act, 1956, for the purpose of this paper, provisions of the extant law i.e. the Companies Act, 2013 are referred to.

[9]According to section 2(69) of the Companies Act, 2013 the term 'Promoter' has been defined as:

A person who has been named as such in a prospectus or is identified by the company in the annual return in section 92; or

A person who has control over the affairs of the company, directly or indirectly whether as a shareholder, director or otherwise; or

A person who is in agreement with whose advice, directions or instructions the board of directors of the company is accustomed to act.

[10] This is a new requirement in Indian Company law; there were no such restrictions in the previous Company law. For detailed provisions, refer to section 2 (87) of the Companies Act, 2013 read with Companies (Restriction on number of layers) Rules, 2017.

[11] Section 19 of the Companies Act, 2013

[12] Section 129 (3) of the Companies Act, 2013

[13] Sections 136 (1) and 137 (1) of the Companies Act, 2013

[14] Schedule III of the Companies Act, 2013

[15] Section 92 (1) of the Companies Act, 2013

[16] Section 233 of the Companies Act, 2013

[17] Section 2 (37) of the Companies Act, 2013

[18] Section 70 (1) (a) of the Companies Act, 2013

[19] Section 186 (1) of the Companies Act, 2013

[20] Section 149 (6) of the Companies Act, 2013

[21] Section 141 (3) of the Companies Act, 2013

[22] Section 143 (1) of the Companies Act, 2013

[23] Section 144 of the Companies Act, 2013

[24] Section 192 (1) of the Companies Act, 2013

[25] Section 170 (1) of the Companies Act, 2013

[26] Regulation 16 (1) (c) of SEBI LODR Regulations

[27] Regulation 33 and Schedule IV of SEBI LODR Regulations

[28] Regulation 16 (1) (b) of SEBI LODR Regulations

[29] Regulations 24, read with Schedule II, 24A, 30 read with Schedule III, 37, 46 (2) (s) and Schedule V of SEBI LODR Regulations.

[30] SEBI Circular dated May 10, 2018, available at the following link: https://www.sebi.gov.in/legal/circulars/may-2018/circular-for-implementation-of-certain-recommendations-of-the-committee-on-corporate-governance-under-the-chairmanship-of-shri-uday-kotak_38905.html

[31] In addition to the persons included as 'related parties' as defined in SEBI Regulations, a person or entity belonging to the promoter or promoter group of the listed entity and holding 20% or more of the shareholding in the listed entity is deemed to be a related party.

[32] https://www.sebi.gov.in/reports/reports/oct-2017/report-of-the-committee-on-corporate-governance_36177.html

[33] http://www.doingbusiness.org/en/data/exploreeconomies/india

[34] Format of the annual return (Form MGT-7) is prescribed under section 92 (1) of the Companies Act, 2013, available at the following link: http://www.mca.gov.in/MinistryV2/companyformsdownload.html

[35] Schedule III of the Companies Act, 2013

[36] Regulation 31 of SEBI LODR Regulations along-with SEBI Circulars dated November 30, 2015 (https://www.sebi.gov.in/legal/circulars/nov-2015/disclosure-of-holding-of-specified-securities-and-holding-of-specified-securities-in-dematerialized-form_31140.html) read with Circulars dated December 07, 2018 (https://www.sebi.gov.in/legal/circulars/dec-2018/disclosure-of-significant-beneficial-ownership-in-the-shareholding-pattern_41245.html) and March 12, 2019 (https://www.sebi.gov.in/legal/circulars/mar-2019/modification-of-circular-dated-december-7-2018-on-disclosure-of-significant-beneficial-ownership-in-the-shareholding-pattern_42324.html)

[37] Refer to rules relating to significant beneficial ownership under Companies Act, 2013, available at the following links: http://www.mca.gov.in/Ministry/pdf/CompaniesOwnersAmendmentRules_08020219.pdf and http://www.mca.gov.in/Ministry/pdf/CompaniesSignificantRules_01072019.pdf

[38] Schedule III of Companies Act, 2013.

[39] For detailed provisions for related party transactions under Companies Act, 2013, refer to sections 2(76), 177 (4) and 188 of the Companies Act, 2013.

[40] For detailed provisions for related party transactions under SEBI LODR Regulations, refer to regulation 23 and part A of Schedule V of SEBI LODR Regulations.

[41] Sections 179, 185, 186 and Schedule III of the Companies Act, 2013.

4 Case study on Israel

This chapter on Israel describes the prevalence of company groups in the Israeli economy and among its listed companies which reached a peak a decade ago. Despite high corporate governance standards, such market structure raised concern regarding various potential risks related to pyramidal holdings, separation between the control of significant financial and non-financial corporations and other characteristics of company groups in Israel. The chapter highlights that major corporate governance reforms, along with structural reforms that addressed these risks, have dramatically decreased the size and dominance of company groups, facilitating stronger safeguards for minority shareholder protection, and enhancing enforcement, especially private.

Introduction

Company groups are a prevalent phenomenon in Israel, as in many other countries. Historically, a large majority of the companies listed on the Tel-Aviv Stock Exchange ("**TASE**") had a controlling shareholder, and major segments of the Israeli market were controlled by a relatively small number of company groups.

Company groups differ greatly in size, ownership structure, organisational structure and businesses included in the group. It should be noted that it is very common to have both listed and unlisted companies in the same group. Private companies may be holding companies or subsidiaries depending on the group structure. Company groups may have significant advantages for shareholders ("SH") value and to the economy due to scale and cross-benefits of businesses in different sectors, but there may also be disadvantages, both on economy level (i.e. concentration and competition concerns) and on the individual company level (complex agency problems between the controlling SH and minority SH through in different companies in the group).

From a corporate governance point of view there is no single comprehensive law in Israel regarding company groups. Israeli corporate governance is mainly designed to cope with the agency and other problems characterising controlled companies. For example, the Israeli Companies Law—1999 ("**ICL**") deals with corporate governance issues like board composition and approval procedures for related party transactions ("**RPT**"), including majority of minority ("**MOM**") vote. The Israeli Securities Law—1968 ("**ISL**") deals with relevant disclosure and the accounting regime. Such provisions of course apply to company groups as well and are very important for their governance, as will be described below.

The last decade has seen major reforms in Israeli law aimed to curb the negative effects of company groups both on economy level and on corporate governance level. These reforms strengthened minority protection in public companies, mainly regarding RPTs and remuneration, curbed the size of company groups and imposed restrictions on integration of different businesses under one company group.

Structural reform

The Committee on Increasing Competitiveness in the Israeli Economy

In 2010 the Israeli Government appointed the "Committee on Increasing Competitiveness in the Israeli Economy" ("**the Committee**"). The Committee published an interim report in 2011 and its final report in 2012.

The Committee was concerned, regarding company groups in Israel, that an overwhelming majority (88%) of the companies publicly traded in TASE had a controlling shareholder. The committee found that there were 28 company groups, which constituted 25% of all public companies. The Committee also found that a majority of the market capitalisation of those companies was held by company groups (54%). Controlled publicly traded companies were the "building stones" of company groups and in more than a third of them, the controlling shareholder invested less than 50% of the capital. The prevalent holding structure was pyramidal—in 79% of the groups the structure contained at least two layers of publicly-traded companies. The Committee also found that 58% of the company groups had three or more pyramidal tiers—there were more than 70 companies in the third layers and above. The market value of listed companies in the third layer and above was 14% of the market value of all the companies listed in TASE and was estimated at 100 billion NIS.

Additionally, the Committee found that the average control premium in Israel was among the highest in the world—about 27%, which was more than double the global average and almost three times the OECD weighted average. The Committee found this indicative of a non-efficient control market thus raising concerns regarding minority protection. The Committee observed that agency problems become more severe as the "wedge" between the controller cash flow and voting rights increases. The committee found evidence that private benefits in Israel are high compared to international levels, indicating that agency problems and extraction of private benefits need more regulatory attention.

The Committee indicated that a pyramid structure enabled a controller to circumvent the mandatory rule of "one share one vote" applying to publicly listed companies by section 46B of the ISL, thus enabling control of subsidiaries with a relatively small capital investment.

The Committee also found that the structure of the economy in Israel, from the supra-sector aspect, was centralised, with a small number of individuals controlling a significant portion of the real and financial assets in the economy by means of business groups. The Committee noted that the complexity and the degree of leverage in business groups, in the regulatory situation and structure of the economy then existing, increased the risks at the economy level to the financial system's robustness and to the protection of depositor or investor interests.

The Committee also observed that competition between few groups in several different markets may lead to inefficiency in the specific markets as the group may maximise profit on a group level and not on a company level, hence derogating competition in the relevant markets. This risk increases when there is a financial institution in the group as it is exposed to data from many markets as its customers and thus information symmetry is hindered and allocation of credit by such financial institutions may be inefficient. When groups are major consumers of debt and also control a financial institution, this might cause a systemic risk to market stability. It should also be noted that financial institutions play an important role in the corporate governance of listed firms as direct or indirect minority SH through customers' holdings.

The Committee's recommendations were intended to cope with these potential risks in three aspects—restriction of the height (or number of layers) of pyramidal holdings; separation of control over significant real holdings and significant financial holdings; and obligation to consider economy-wide centralisation when allocating public assets through licensing, privatisation, etc.

The recommendations were chosen to be structural due to three main reasons. First, it was observed that there is a limit to the effectiveness of corporate governance rules when agency problems and conflict of interests are severe. Secondly, market and systemic risks as opposed to company-related risks are not effectively managed by corporate governance alone. Third, regarding the size of pyramidal holding groups, structural rules are clearer to follow and enforce than rules based on the "wedge" between cash flow and voting rights, even though the rationale for limiting the size of such groups is based on its implications.

The Committee expected that implementing its recommendations will improve the efficiency of the allocation of resources, make a positive contribution to the stability of the financial system and support the growth of the economy and the welfare of the public in the middle and long term.

Enactment of LPCRC

The Law for the Promotion of Competition and Reduction of Concentration ("**LPCRC**") was enacted on 11 December 2013 following the Committee's recommendations. LPCRC aims to increase market competition and sectorial competition; decrease the level of market concentration; and simplify the corporate group structure and decentralise their control in the market.

LPCRC defines "a group of holders" as "a corporation, a controlling shareholder of a corporation or a corporation controlled by either of them". This definition is used to prevent evasion from the law provisions by division of the holdings among different corporations included in the group. Similarly, this law defines "control" regarding a pyramid group by attributing all the group holdings to the controlling company.

The law is divided into three main parts which will be briefly presented below.

Pyramidal holding structures

One part of the law is aimed at limiting pyramids as a means of control. Pyramidal structures were required to be dismantled to a two "layer" structure, and new pyramidal structures may not consist of more than two "layers". A "layer company" is a company which has shares or debt listed on TASE (excluding privately owned companies).

This limitation came into full effect at the end of 2019.

Separation of control over significant financial institutions and significant real companies

Another part of the LPCRC was designed to separate the ownership of significant financial institutions from significant real companies. LPCRC forbids a significant real company (whether listed or not) or its controlling entity to control any significant financial corporations (whether listed or not) or to hold more than 10% of any kind of means of control[1] in such entity. In addition, a person that holds more than 5% of any kind of means of control in a significant real company cannot control significant financial corporations. Control or excess holdings in violation of these percentages must be sold and such sale may be forced by appointment of a receiver by Court at the regulator's request.

Furthermore, to prevent conflict of interest on a personal basis, the law forbids a person to be a director or an executive in both significant real and significant financial corporations, or to be nominated as a director or executive in a significant real corporation if its relative[2], its partner or a person with whom he has labour relationship, business or professional relationship holds such position in a significant financial corporation (or vice versa). This applies to independent directors as well, even if the real and financial companies are not in the same company group.

This limitation came into full effect at the end of 2019.

Allocation of public assets

A third part of the law is divided into two main provisions.

The first provision deals with the obligation of a government ministry seeking to allocate public assets (licenses, contracts or shares in essential infrastructures and in the privatisation of government companies) to "concentrated entities" to take into consideration, in consultation with a specialised Committee, the level of economy-wide concentration. "Concentrated entities" are defined as significant real companies; significant financial corporations; and media groups.

The second provision of this part of the law obligates any government ministry seeking to allocate a right to a private entity, to take into consideration the "promotion of industry specific competition". This obligation applies to rights that involve contracts or significant holdings of essential infrastructures or a license (even if it is not for an essential infrastructure) and on the condition that due to the nature of the right, its economic value or the law that applies to it, the number of operators in the relevant industry is limited.

These provisions are intended to promote competition on a multi-market level, reduce concentration of economic power in a few hands and curb potential political influence of huge company groups.

Corporate governance reform

Background

As was mentioned above, the "company group theory", where the separate personality of each company in the group is ignored and the group is treated as one economic entity— was never adopted into Israeli company law. Like in other legal systems influenced by common law, the approach of the ICL regarding corporate governance and board duties is based upon the theory of separate legal personality of the corporation. The ICL views each and every company as a separate legal entity. Directors' duties are to act in the interests of the company whose board they serve on. The interest of the company is defined to operate in accordance with business considerations to maximise its profits.

From a subsidiary point of view the meaning is that the board must act independently, even if the company is part of a controlled group. From a parent company point of view the subsidiary is an asset of the parent, and the parent company is expected to maximise its asset's value. Nevertheless, the parent company cannot force the board of its subsidiary to adopt a certain policy or to make a specific decision. The ICL enables a parent company to act as a shareholder in the GM to dismiss directors (section 230(a)) or in extreme cases even to assume powers (and duties) conferred on another organ (section 50).

The ICL stresses the duty of a director to exercise independent judgment. A director who violates his duty to exercise independent judgment will be deemed as breaching his fiduciary duties. In the 2011 amendment 16 to ICL added provisions forbidding any person from performing duties of a director unless duly appointed as such, nor interfere in a director's independent judgment. Violation of this rule will expose such person to full duties and liabilities of a director (section 106). Therefore, in a group context, if directors of a parent company interfere in the management of the subsidiary, they may be seen as shadow directors who owe fiduciary duty and a duty of care to the subsidiary (section 106). Such situations can also lead a court to pierce the corporate veil, following which a Court may attribute a debt of the subsidiary to the parent company (section 6). It should be noted though that piercing the corporate veil is limited to exceptional and extreme cases, where the separate legal personality is being misused fraudulently.

An example to the application of the new provision of section 106 can be found in a recent case involving an insurance company which is part of a company group. The insurance company was a private company held by a public holding company. The parent board intended to institute a board committee that will monitor the subsidiary (the insurance company). The regulator was concerned that this is an unacceptable attempt to interfere with management of the insurance company and considered taking regulatory measures against the decision. Following the regulatory concern, as well as a private lawsuit[3] filed in the matter, the parent company revised its decision and decided not to establish the aforementioned committee.

Relevant definitions

There is no single legal definition of a company group in Israeli law. There are relevant definitions regarding control and subsidiaries.

The ISL defines "**control**" as the ability to direct the activity of a corporation, excluding an ability deriving merely from holding an office of director or another office in the corporation. A person shall be presumed a **"control holder"** if he or she holds half or more of a certain type of means of control of the corporation. This definition has both a qualitative and quantitative dimension. Shareholders who are relatives or connected by a voting agreement or an agreement for the appointment of all directors may be regarded together as control holders.

A "**subsidiary**" is defined as a company in which another company holds 50% or more of the nominal value of its issued share capital, of the voting power therein or is entitled to appoint half or more of the directors or its general manager. Similar definitions are also included in ICL.

The ISL also defines a broader relation to a "**related company**", which is a company in which another company— which is not a parent company— has invested an amount equal to 25% or more of the equity of the other company; or a company in which another company— which is not a parent company— holds 25% or more of the par value of its issued share capital or of its voting power, or may appoint 25% or more of its directors.

The securities regulations stipulate that, in general, an issuer must disclose its business, including its financial information, on a group level. The term "group" is defined as including the corporation, joint project (engagement for carrying out economic activity that materially affects the corporation's profitability, its property, or obligations), and material companies that are under its control.

Minority protection in a company group environment

The ICL and ISL contain special provisions designed to address the unique challenges which derive from the Israeli market structure (concentrated holdings; companies groups; pyramids) as will be further described.

A main goal of the Israeli legal framework is to provide adequate minority protection and address agency problems between minority shareholders and the controller, which is aggravated in a company group.

As mentioned above, LPCRC provisions regarding pyramidal holding groups were aimed to prevent the use of such structures to circumvent the rule of "one share one vote" that is enacted in ISL (section 46B).

Board composition and board committees

A basic aspect of governance requirements in public companies are provisions aimed at maintaining a degree of independence at the board level, in order to strengthen its ability to effectively monitor the management. ICL requires at least two "outside directors" in a public company (sec 239).

An outside director is strongly independent from the controller. This is achieved both by independence criteria and appointment procedure. Independence criteria is examined on a group level, requiring independence not only from the company point of view but also from controller and any company controlled by him or her (sec. 240). Appointment procedure requires that an outside director be appointed by a general meeting vote requiring MOM approval for a set three-year tenure (and can be appointed by MOM approval for two consecutive tenures) (Sec 245).

In practice, a public company usually appoints at least one more independent director. An "independent director" must comply with the same independence requirements but is appointed like other directors. There is no obligation to appoint independent directors except the "outside directors" and directors qualifying for board committees (see below). But in 2011 a recommended corporate governance provision was added to the ICL stating that in a company in which there is a controlling shareholder at least one third of the directors shall be independent directors (when there is no controlling SH the recommendation is for a majority of independent directors).

The composition of the mandatory board committees is designed to preserve their independence.

The audit committee is responsible for reviewing flaws in the management of the company, supervising the internal auditor, overviewing whistle-blower protection and approving several aspects of RPTs. The committee must include all the "outside directors" and a majority of independent directors. The rest of the members must comply with independence criteria to make sure they are not affiliated to the group: "The following shall not serve as members of an audit committee: The chairman of the board of directors and any director employed by the company or employed by the controlling shareholder thereof or by a corporation controlled by such controlling shareholder, a director providing services, on a regular basis, to the company or to a corporation controlled by a controlling shareholder as aforementioned, as well as a director whose primary income is dependent on the controlling shareholder" (sec. 115). This requirement is referred to in the market as "light independence".

The financial statements committee must be headed by an "outside director" and the rest of its members need to qualify for "light independence". Other requirements deal with financial literacy and will not be discussed here (Regulations according to sec. 171(E)).

The remuneration committee should include a majority of outside directors, and its other members must qualify for "light independence" and be remunerated according to the limitations regarding "outside directors" (Sec 118A).

It should be noted that law reforms in 2011 made the independence criteria more stringent (sec 240(B) and (F)); enhanced the independence of the audit committee (sec 115) and established the even more independent remuneration committee (sec 118A).

Separation of CEO and chairperson positions

The ICL stipulates that the CEO and his or her relative may not be appointed as the chairperson of the board and an individual, who is subordinate to the CEO, directly or indirectly, may not be appointed as the chairperson unless approved by a MOM vote.

The chairperson or his or her relative may also not be assigned duties of the CEO or of a subordinate of the CEO. The chairperson of the board in a public company may not serve in any position in the company or a company controlled by it, except director or chairperson of the board in the controlled company.

Before amendment 16 to the ICL in 2011 this rule applied only to the CEO himself.

MOM approval

The main protection to minority SHs in ICL is by requiring certain transactions or issues to be approved, inter alia, by a majority of SH that includes a majority of the minority shareholders, excluding any minority votes held by a SH related to the controller (MOM approval as defined above):

1. Transactions with a controlling shareholder which is extraordinary (sec. 270 (4)). The provisions regarding RPTs are discussed below.
2. Remuneration—the company's remuneration policy is set by the remuneration committee and should be approved by MOM approval (Sec. 267A, 272). In addition, any remuneration agreement that is not in accordance with that policy and any remuneration agreement with the CEO must be approved by MOM as well as the CEO remuneration. The vote on those matters is not binding, with the exception of remuneration of a director or for the controller who serves as a director or executive. The amendment to ICL regarding remuneration policy and transactions was enacted in 2013 and will not be described in detail in this paper.
3. Merger—a merger between a public company and another company controlled by the same controller (i.e. in the same group) requires, inter alia, MOM approval (sec 320).
4. Appointment of "Outside Directors" as described above.

Related party transactions

RPTs may in some cases be beneficial to the company, but in other cases may be abusive at the expense of the minority SHs. RPTs involve conflict of interest, or agency problem, and therefore require approval processes stipulated in the ICL.

An entire chapter in the ICL is dedicated to the approval processes of different types of RPTs involving directors, managers or controlling shareholders. The ICL requires a mandatory approval process in advance (ex-ante). A precondition for the approval of an RPT is that the transaction is in the company's interest, and is not valid unless approved according to the requirements in the law. Other requirements in the ICL as well as case law imply that the conditions of an RPT transaction should be fair and when relevant, in similar terms to a parallel transaction between unrelated parties, as will be further discussed below.

In the context of company groups the main focus of ICL is on transactions with the controlling SH, or with a third party if the controlling SH has a personal interest in it. Such transactions include remuneration agreements (section 270 (4)).

For the purpose of transactions with interested parties, the definition of 'controlling shareholder' has been expanded and it also includes a holder of 25% or more of the voting rights in the company's general meeting if there is no other person holding more than 50% of the voting rights in the company (section 268).

It should be noted that this provision is interpreted as also including transactions of a private subsidiary with the controller of the public company. Such transactions will require the same approval in the public company as if it entered it itself, in order not to circumvent legislative purpose.

The audit committee is required to classify every RPT (or class of RPTs) as either an extraordinary transaction, non-extraordinary or negligible (sec. 117(1A)). A transaction is defined as extraordinary if it is either not in the company's regular course of business; not undertaken in market conditions; or if it is likely to materially influence the profitability of the company, its property or liabilities (Section 1).

Approval of extraordinary RPTs requires three stages: first approval by the audit committee; then the board of directors; and at last the GM in a majority vote requiring also MOM[4] (Section 275).

Until 2011 (amendment 16 to the ICL) the MOM vote required only 1/3 of the minority vote. Another reform in 2011 required that a transaction with a controlling shareholder for a period of over three years should be re-approved every three years (Section 275).[5] These new provisions had a huge effect on approval of RPTs and gave greater power to minority SHs to review and approve the terms of the transaction periodically. This may be seen together with new research described below that indicates decline of control premium in Israel as indication to further enhance and improve minority protection in Israel.

In 2013 amendment 22 to the ICL prescribed that the audit committee set forth a procedure for entering a RPT which should include a competitive procedure or a different procedure to be conducted prior to engaging in the transaction. This requirement is intended to approximate market terms or to ensure that the transaction is in the benefit of the company (Section 275).

MOM approval does not prevent judicial review ex-post if a transaction is later contested in court. Generally, courts reviewing RPTs will uphold them to entire fairness standard (See: C.A 2718/09 Gadish Kranot Tagmulim v. Elsint (Nevo, 28.5.2012); Cls. Act. 26809-01-11 Kahana v. Machteshim Agan Taasiyot (Nevo, 15.5.2011)). However, in some cases where the board appointed an independent committee to negotiate the transaction, and if the negotiations were real and honest and on a fully informed basis, the court may uphold the contested transaction to the Israeli version of the Business Judgement Rule (BJR) (See for instance: Cls. Act.43859-08-13 Segal Levy Yizum and Nekhasim v. Kur Taasiyot (Nevo, 9.1.2014)). The practice that has been established following those rulings is to institute such committees to negotiate major RPTs. This practice was not included in the ICL.

The judicial review may result in practice the courts declaring the transaction or parts of it void or determining the 'fair value' of the consideration. It can also result in holding executives and directors in breach of their fiduciary duties or duty of care.

Approval of a non-extraordinary RPT: the audit committee is required to determine an adequate approval procedure inside the company. Such procedure should include a competitive procedure or a different procedure to be conducted prior to engaging in the transaction. This requirement is intended to approximate market terms or to ensure that the transaction is in the benefit of the company (Section 117 (1B); Section 117 (2A)).

Negligible RPTs do not require special approval procedures but are subject to accumulative disclosure. The audit committee must determine the manner of approval of transactions that are not negligible, including determining types of transactions that will require the approval of the audit committee. The audit committee may decide on such classification for a type of transaction, according to criteria to be determined once a year in advance.

Another condition for approval of an RPT is that the audit committee and the board check whether the transaction includes distribution of dividend or self-purchase of shares. In such cases the rules regarding distribution of profits apply as well.

Enforcement

An additional layer of minority SH protection is **administrative and private enforcement** mechanisms. Private enforcement will lead to judicial review, inter alia, of RPT and many other issues, mainly in form of class action or a derivative suit. In the last decade such enforcement rose dramatically, much of it attributed to the establishment of a specialised court as described below.

With regard to company groups it should be mentioned that in 2014 the Israeli Supreme Court recognised the right of a shareholder in a public company to file a multi-derivative suit, i.e. on behalf of a subsidiary or a subsidiary of a subsidiary, under the same chain of control.[6]

In 2010 legislation introduced new specialised judicial forums—the Economic Department of the Tel Aviv District Court (which was practically established in 2011) for corporate and securities litigation, as well as the Administrative Enforcement Committee, which facilitated enhanced administrative enforcement by ISA of both ICL corporate governance rules and securities law.

Enhanced enforcement and specialised court decisions both made significant contributions to company group governance through better enforcement of RPT requirements. The ISA and the Attorney General take an active role providing expert opinions to the courts and funding selected SH suits.

Relevant case law—Fiduciary duties

Fiduciary duties of the board of directors in group context were contested more than once in Israeli courts, usually during derivative suits or class actions. Here are several main examples from case law.

In Der. Act. 10466-09-12 Ostrovski v. DIC (9.8.2015), a derivative suit was filed against the board of directors of DIC, a public holding company which was then a third tier in a multi-tier group. The major claim was that the board has breached its duty of care by approving an acquisition sought by the controller of Maariv, a media company, as well as extension of credit to Maariv following the acquisition. This investment ended up in huge losses and the plaintiff argued it was made as per the request of the controller without sufficient information and examination. The derivative suit ended in a settlement.

In C.A 773/14 Vardenikov v. Alovich (30.11.2015) a derivative suit was filed against the board of Bezek (a public telecom company) claiming that the company's distribution and debt financing policies were not in the company's interest but rather the controller's interest to pay his personal debts after a LBO of the company. The board invoked the BJR and the court accepted and dismissed the case.

In Der. Act. 37473-09-12 Ben Israel v. Dankner (18.11.2015) a derivative suit was filed against both the board of directors and the controller, according to which they were in conflict of interest when approving an acquisition of another company from a private company held by the controller. Following the contested acquisition, the controller was relieved from financial obligations to the purchased company. The transaction was claimed to be in the interest of the controller and other companies at his control but not in the interest of the acquiring public company. Proceedings ended on a settlement.

Another line of cases which are related to fiduciary duties deals with allocation of business opportunities. Courts held that director's fiduciary duties forbid them from taking advantage of business opportunities related to the company's business, even if the company is not in a position to take advantage of that opportunity itself (see in re 25351-01-12 Hatahana Hamerkazit Be Tel Aviv v. Nitzba Hakhzakot (22.8.2017); Der.Act 20136-09-12 Biton v. Pangaya Nadlan (21.10.2013)).

Relevant case law—Company groups

Several examples from rich case law demonstrate how corporate governance flaws in company groups are addressed.

The case of Melisron LTD (Criminal Appeal 99/14) dealt with a company group were the defendants served as officers in several companies in the group, both private and public. The Supreme Court determined that if a person serves as an organ in several companies in a company group, and the entire company groups acted as one economic unit and had a uniform economic purpose then each company may be convicted on the basis of the organ's actions.

In Shahar Hamillenium LTD case (Criminal Appeal 5836/16, 6210/16) a public company and the controller were convicted of fraud and reporting offenses due to cash withdrawal by a controlling public company from its public subsidiary was concealed from the board and the public by the controller and the CFO and not duly approved.

Administrative Enforcement by ISA dealt, inter alia, with cases where financial statements of subsidiaries where not consolidated into the parent company's statements (Administrative Case 1/12 Mivtach Shamir LTD[7]) and failure to report a delay in payment of a loan given to the controller (Administrative Case 3/13 Inventech Central Hotels LTD[8]).

Disclosure and the right to information

The ICL defines a strong right of SHs to information relevant to any issue discussed in the GM (Section 184-186). In public companies this right is usually realised through disclosure under ISL.

The ISL requires a public company to disclose any material information regarding its activity to the ISA and to the public. This rule also applies to information regarding a private company that is considered to be of material importance to the public company (where both companies belong to the same group).

This is further reinforced by IAS 24 disclosure requirements applying to related parties within company groups. Contractual agreements between a public company or its subsidiaries and affiliated companies in the group, that are substantial for the public company, must be disclosed in detail.

In addition, the regulatory framework addresses disclosure of more aspects of ownership and control in company groups.

The Securities Regulations (Periodic and Immediate Reports) 1970, provide a list of events which require immediate disclosure[9]. These are events deemed material by the legislator in every reporting corporation, for example:

1. **Changes in the holdings of certain interested parties:** Immediate disclosure regarding a person who has ceased or has become an interested party in the corporation, as well as changes in his holdings. The disclosing obligation also applies to the interested party whose holdings have undergone a reportable change.

2. "An interested party in a corporation" is defined as (1) A person who holds 5% or more of the issued share capital of the corporation or of the voting rights therein, whoever is entitled to appoint one or more directors of the corporation or its general manager, whoever serves as a director of the corporation or its general manager, or a corporation in which such person holds 25% or more of its issued share capital or of the voting power therein, or may appoint 25% or more of its directors; (2) a subsidiary of a corporation, except a registration company.
3. In addition, a corporation is required to publish the existence of voting agreements and other agreements relating to the holding of the corporation's securities.
4. **Disclosure of specific transactions:** several regulations focus on disclosure relating to specific transactions, such as: a private placement of securities, a transaction between a company and the controlling shareholder, a tender offer, a merger, and offering of securities to the public.
5. **Remuneration**: disclosure should be provided regarding all components of the terms of office of directors, officers and controlling shareholders who serve as office holder in the company, which require approval of the general meeting, even in cases that such approval is not required due to a specific relief in Regulations (i.e. due to minor changes).
6. Details of remuneration should also be disclosed for: (a) five highest remuneration among officers and directors of the corporation or its subsidiary; (b) three senior officers with the highest remuneration in the corporation if not included in (a) above; (c) any interested party in the corporation not listed in paragraphs (a) or (b).

In the annual report[10], a corporation is required to mention the name of its controlling shareholder, if control was transferred during the period described in the report and the name of the person who was the controlling shareholder of the corporation during that period.

In addition, the report must mention the shares and other securities that each interested party in the corporation holds in the corporation on the date of the report or on a date as close to it as possible, detailing the name of each interested party, the rate at which he holds the shares and each of the other securities of the corporation which the corporation undertook to sell to him.

Furthermore, in the annual report a corporation is required to report all its transactions with the controlling shareholder or in which the controlling shareholder has a personal interest during the last two years, or which are in effect at the date of the report.

However, a company is not obligated to report transactions that are considered negligible, as long as the company has determined the types and characteristics of negligible transactions. In practice, a "best practice" was created for this matter, according to which companies approved in advance a procedure for classifying negligible transactions while determining the relevant parameters according to the type of transaction, both qualitatively and quantitatively.

In addition, the annual report must include a list of the corporation's financial position in each of the subsidiaries and affiliates companies and specify the changes in the corporation's investments in the reporting year in each subsidiary and in its affiliated company, including the dates of the changes and the main terms of the transactions related to these changes. The specification should also relate to changes in a company that became a subsidiary or affiliate, or ceased to be such a company in the reporting year.

Moreover, a corporation is required to disclose any material legal proceeding in which any of the directors, office-holders, related companies or interested parties are a counter-party to the corporation or who have an interest in that proceeding which is contrary to the interest of the corporation.

Control premium

As mentioned above, a high control premium in Israel was seen as a major indicator for market concentration and corporate governance deficiencies in the country.

It is interesting to see the change in control premium in Israel a decade later, mainly attributed by researchers to the effect of the LPCRC and the amendments to ICL, especially the requirement that a transaction with a controlling shareholder for a period of over three years should be re-approved every three years.

A famous study by Dyck & Zingales examined the average level of the control premium in 39 developed countries by estimating how much a new controlling shareholder pays above market price in control transactions. The study examined control transactions between 1990 and 2000. According to this study, Israel's average control premium rate was one of the highest in the world, about 27%, almost twice as high as the global average of 14%.[11] In the most advanced capital markets such as the United States and the United Kingdom, the control premium rate was even lower and stood at 3% or less.

These studies have greatly influenced the decision makers in Israel and led to a long list of reforms in the Companies Law and the Securities Law. The main reforms are described above. They were intended, inter alia, to reduce the negative effects reflected in the high control premium in Israel.

New research conducted by Professor Sharon Hannes and Mr. Eylon Blum had initial data published that might indicate a major change in control premium. The initial data from this research includes control transactions in the highest listing segment in TASE during 2006-2014. The study included 13 transactions, in which the average control premium was only 4.6%— a significant decrease in two decades. Moreover, the weighted average calculated according to the size of the transactions was a premium of only 1.2%. In five out of the 13 transactions examined there was a negative premium. But the median control premium in transactions with a positive premium was 10.3%.[12]

These initial research findings may indicate a significant change of trend in control premium. These findings should be looked at together with several recent occasions where controllers decided to dissolve their control and sell their controlling shares in the company in the stock exchange (Paz, Discount Bank, Poalim Bank, etc.). Therefore, at the same time, and probably not coincidentally, we are experiencing a decline in the proportion of companies that have controlling shareholders towards more decentralised control structures.

This trend of companies with decentralised ownership has also changed the regulatory concerns in MOJ and ISA with respect to governance and duties of board in company groups. Historically and as mentioned above, the major concerns were regarding controlling shareholder, RPTs and board independence. Today, regulatory concerns shift also to board effectiveness, board–management relationship and the implications on institutional investors' engagement. In companies where there is no controlling SH, it is important to have an independent, strong and professional board of directors, with an active supervisory circle of caring and involved shareholders. MOJ is currently conducting research aimed to amend the ICL and add provisions relevant to non-controlled companies.

Recent data on company groups in Israel

By the end of 2017, four years after the enactment of LPCRC and two years before it comes to full effect, and six years after major reforms regarding RPTs in the ICL the share of controlled companies in TASE declined from 88% to 80%. The number of company groups declined mildly to 26 company groups, which include 23% of all public companies, and their share in market capitalisation declined from 54% to 35% of the value of the stock exchange market. In the end of 2018, only eight companies remain in the third tier of pyramidal groups, and the market value of these eight companies is only 3.7% of market capitalisation (estimated at 26 billion NIS). The company groups including these companies were required to comply with the two-layer rule of LPCRC by December 2019.

It should also be mentioned that three out of the five largest banks in Israel, were part of a company group comprising of both significant financial banking activities and significant real holdings. To date, no bank is part of such group.

In addition, the two last insurance companies that were still part of company groups with both significant real and financial holdings have ceased such status before December 2019— in one case by acquisition by a different controller and in another case by dissolving control and selling the controlling shares to the public.

Conclusions

In the last decade Israel enacted several reforms which had dramatic influence on company groups and corporate governance in controlled companies.

These reforms aimed to promote competitiveness and efficient allocation of capital and to minimise systemic risks deriving from the structure of the market at that time. These reforms also aimed to protect investors in public companies and minimise agency problems in controlled companies.

It is early to assess the impact of all these reforms but even now some significant trends can be noted – decrease in the size and dominance of company groups in the Israeli market; enhanced enforcement, especially private, which contributes to higher standards of corporate governance and a decrease of control premium that may indicate more effective investor protection and fewer opportunities to extract private benefits of control. In addition, several recent cases where controllers decided to dissolve their control may indicate an initial trend of more companies with decentralised control structures.

References

OECD (2015), *G20/OECD Principles of Corporate Governance*, OECD Publishing, Paris, https://doi.org/10.1787/9789264236882-en.

Blum, Eylon and Hannes, Sharon (2016), Does Law Matter? Private Benefits of the Controlling Shareholder Following Legal Reform, http://web.law.columbia.edu/sites/default/files/microsites/law-economics-studies/control_premiun_cls.pdf

Notes

[1] For this purpose, "Means of control" are broadly defined as any of the following: (1) the right to vote at a general meeting of a company or of a parallel body of another body corporate; (2) The right to appoint a director in a corporation; (3) the right to participate in the profits of the corporation; (4) the right to the balance of the corporation's assets upon its liquidation after the discharge of its liabilities.

[2] "Relative": a spouse, brother, parent, descendant, descendant of the spouse, and spouse of any of the above.

[3] The lawsuit was filed by one of the shareholders in the public holding company. The shareholder claimed, against the two companies and the three directors who were appointed to be members of the committee, that the institution of the committee should not be permitted. The shareholder asked the court for declaratory reliefs according to which there is no legal or corporate validity for the institution of the board of directors committee, and also that the board of directors committee is not entitled to instruct or guide officers in the insurance company and accordingly officers in the insurance company are not permitted to act in accordance with its instructions or guidance.

[4] The transaction will be approved, even without MOM approval, if shareholders voting against the transaction represent less than 2% of the voting SHs.

[5] A relief in regulations allows a company which offers its securities to the public for the first time (IPO) re-approve such a transaction only five years after the IPO if it was duly described in the offering prospectus.

[6] See: C.A.R. 2903/13 Iterkoloni Hashkaot v. Shmuel Shkedi (Nevo, 27.08.2014).

[7] Mivtach Shamir is a public company that, together with Apax funds, acquired 76% of the shares of the Tnuva Group, a private company. Mivtach Shamir was required by ISA to describe its investment in Tnuva in the periodic reports, as required by the Securities Regulations, and to attach the reports of the holding corporation and the Tnuva Group's reports. The Administrative Enforcement Committee approved an enforcement arrangement, and stated that a private corporation, held by a public corporation is obligated to disclose information to the holding parent company as if it was its own obligations.

[8] Despite the fact that the controlling shareholder did not repay the loan on time, the Company did not report it. Later the controlling shareholder demanded that the Company return part of the repayment amount and, in fact, received a new loan from the company. This transaction was also not reported to the public. The Administrative Enforcement Committee regarded the case as a severe flaw in corporate governance, and regarded the company officers' actions as breach of duties and action in conflict of interest.

[9] The immediate reports are published upon the occurrence of a material event on the day such event occurred or on the first trading day following the occurrence of such event (depending on the time such material information relating to its affairs becomes known to the corporation).

[10] An annual report is submitted once a year and describes the operations of the corporation during previous year. The annual report is submitted within three months as of its reporting year-end.

[11] A. Dyck, & L. Zingales Private benefits of control: An international comparison. *Journal of Finance* 59, 537-600 (2004). In another study by Lauterbach & Ronen, the control premium was calculated for transfer of control transactions in 1993-2005. Their findings revealed a similar picture, according to which the control premium in Israel was 31.5% (B. Lauterbach, & B. Ronen *Estimating the private benefits of control from block trades: methodology and evidence*, EFA 2007 Ljubljana Meetings Paper (2007)). The Economic Department of the Israel Securities Authority, examined the control premium between 2006-2010, and found that the average control premium ranged between 19%-30%.

[12] http://web.law.columbia.edu/sites/default/files/microsites/law-economics-studies/control_premiun_cls.pdf. This study has subsequently been updated and expanded to cover a larger selection of companies and transactions from 2001 -2019, and is available in Hebrew on the Tel Aviv University website (Eylon Blum, Sharon Hannes, Beni Lauterbach and Revital Yoseph, 2020).

5 Case study on Korea

This chapter describes the important role of conglomerates in the Korean economy and capital markets. It notes their vital contribution to Korean economic growth, while also citing concerns related to a range of issues such as risks of unfair intragroup transactions that can impact on investor confidence, requiring governance structures that increase corporate competitiveness while not harming the interests of investors and other stakeholders. It describes the main provisions relevant to the oversight and corporate governance of company groups set out in Korea's regulation on large business groups, the Monopoly Regulation and Fair Trade Act regulation on conglomerates, as well as the Corporate Law. It concludes with a detailed description of relevant proposed legal reforms to the Monopoly Regulation and Fair Trade Act aimed at further improving the Korean legal framework for oversight and corporate governance of company groups.

Introduction

Once a war-torn country, the Republic of Korea has now become the seventh member of OECD 30-50 Club,[1] the group of economies reaching USD 30 000 in per capita income and 50 million in population. Investors around the world are paying keen attention to the Korean companies that have achieved rapid growth, building a global presence. The remarkable accomplishment, however, has been undervalued for so long because of the "Korea Discount," which is caused by weak corporate governance at Korean business groups.

Undeniably, large business groups have played a vital role in the nation's economic growth. Following the Asian Financial Crisis in 1997, however, Korea witnessed increased civic awareness and capital market development. Then, a range of issues at business groups such as unfair intragroup transactions, which had hidden under the growth imperative, was revealed.

In Korea, business groups are very common and make up a large portion of the economy. In an ever-changing business environment, a business group should have a governance structure that increases corporate competitiveness and does not harm the interests of investors and other stakeholders.

This paper is intended to highlight the policy measures taken by Korea in a direction towards strengthening the advantages of a business group system and preventing or at least minimising the side effects. Here, the focus lies on the Corporate Law and the Monopoly Regulation and Fair Trade Act ("Fair Trade Act"). The former deals with matters about corporate governance, and the latter disciplines the behavior of a business group.

The state of play of business groups

Definition of a business group

Article 2 of the Fair Trade Act defines a business group as *a group of companies, the business of which is substantially controlled by the same person*,[2] who may be a company or a natural person. The law sees that the same person controls a company if he/she and a related party owns a combined shareholding of 30% or more as the largest shareholder or can elect half or more of the directors or the representative director. A company belonging to a business group becomes an affiliate of the other companies under the same business group. According to this definition, all companies financed by investors fall under the category of a business group.

Considering the difficulty of effective enforcement, however, "business groups subject to limitations on cross-shareholding" and "business groups subject to disclosure" are separately designated as "conglomerate", limiting the regulatory scope. The respective thresholds for the two business group types are KRW10 trillion or more[3] and KRW5 trillion or more[4] in total assets.

Statistics of business groups[5]

As of May 2019, the Korea Fair Trade Commission ("KFTC") designated 59 business groups as a conglomerate, which collectively have 2 103 member firms under them. Among them, 34 business groups with KRW 10 trillion or more in total assets having 1 421 member companies fall under the category of a "business group subject to limitations on cross-shareholding". Of the 59 conglomerates, a natural person is a controlling shareholder at 51 of them, and a corporate body controls the remaining eight. As at the end of 2018, 25.1% or 196 companies out of the 781 firms listed on the Korea Composite Stock Price Index (KOSPI) market[6] belong to a conglomerate. Their combined market capitalisation is around KRW 914 trillion, or 70% of the entire KOSPI market capitalisation.

The controlling shareholder of a business conglomerate has maintained a controlling power by building a complex shareholding structure, including cross-shareholding. More recently, however, the pyramidal ownership structure is more commonly observed. The change was brought about by the policy efforts to convert a business group into a holding company and eliminate circular shareholding. As a result, circular shareholding has shrunk significantly from 282 cross-shareholding loops at ten business groups in May 2017 to 11 at two business groups in July 2019. As of September 2018, 22 conglomerates, about one-third of the total, elected to become a holding company. Including three intermediate holding companies, 24 holding companies belonging to a conglomerate are listed on KOSPI and own 67 subsidiaries and 21 sub-subsidiaries under them.

Regulation on large business groups

The controlling shareholder at a large business group or conglomerate exerts management control over all member companies. In the meantime, due to a complex ownership structure, the direct economic interest the controlling shareholder has at each affiliated firm varies. To take an example of a company at the lower level of the pyramid, the dividend income finally recognised by the controlling shareholder gets far less, undergoing several steps of the ownership hierarchy. It is so even if the company makes a substantial profit and pays out a handsome amount of dividends. This disparity between control and ownership has an impact on decision-making within the business group. In some cases, there may be a decision unfavorable to a particular company, an excellent example of which is unfair intragroup trading.

Korea's antitrust law attempts to tackle the cause of the problem and thereby to prevent the rise of the control-ownership disparity. Specifically, the law prohibits the business groups subject to cross-shareholding from forming circular shareholding and regulates the behavior of a holding company. The code also tries to deter the potential consequences of the control-ownership disparity by prohibiting tunneling such as intra-group trading. The following details the key provisions of the Monopoly Regulation and Fair Trade Act that deal with large business groups, holding companies, and their corporate governance:

The Monopoly Regulation and Fair Trade Act—Regulation on conglomerates

When a member company of a conglomerate intends to conduct a transaction exceeding a particular scale with an affiliated company or the controlling shareholder, it shall first call a board meeting for a resolution and disclose the purpose of the transaction, trading party, scale and conditions, among others. The threshold is a quarterly transaction reaching 5% of the larger of the company's total capital or capital stock, or KRW 5 billion or more (Article 11(2)).

According to the Financial Investment Services and Capital Markets Act, a listed firm shall disclose the status of the shares held by the directors and substantial shareholders and any change thereof. The Fair Trade Act goes further and imposes a duty to disclose the shares held by the largest and substantial shareholders and any change thereof even on a private member company of a large business group with KRW 10 billion or more in total assets (Article 11(3)).

The Fair Trade Act requires a member firm of a large business group to disclose matters regarding the parent group. The disclosure shall include the status of the member companies' shareholding, their cross/circular shareholding and debt guarantees. It shall further mention whether the business group voted on the shares it acquired or owns in its domestic affiliates (limited to FIs), and transactions with a related party (Article 11(4)).

Concerning the extraction of undue private benefits of control, a member company of a large business group is prohibited from trading with an affiliated firm owned by the controlling shareholder and/or his/her family over a specific ratio[7] and from transferring undue profits to them. According to the data provided by the KFTC, as of May 2018, 231 member companies of a business group were subject to the regulation on the extraction of private benefits of control. At these companies, the controlling shareholder and his/her family held an average of 52.4% of shares. The Fair Trade Act provides the following as acts of transferring undue profits to the controlling shareholder (Article 23(2)):

a. Making a transaction with the related party or affiliate under terms that are substantially more advantageous than terms that have been applied, or deemed to be applied to a deal between unrelated parties.
b. Providing the related party or affiliate with a business opportunity that will bring the company substantial benefits, if it conducts such business directly or through any company controlled by it.
c. Making a transaction of cash or any other financial instrument with the related party under substantially advantageous terms.
d. Making a transaction of a certain scale with the related party or affiliate without giving due consideration to its business ability, financial standing, credit rating and technical power, the price, terms and conditions of the transaction, etc. or without comparing with other business entities.[8]

At the same time, the antitrust law exempts the application of the above provisions to the cases of unquestionable efficiency where the concerned affiliate is part of the supply chain, for example. The rules mentioned above neither apply when there is a risk of technology leakage that potentially causes critical security damage if trading with a party outside the group and when there is an emergency need due to external factors such as a financial crisis.

Furthermore, *a member company of a business group subject to limitations on cross-shareholding with KRW 10 trillion in total assets shall neither acquire nor hold shares of any affiliate that, in turn, acquires or holds shares of that member company.*[9] In case a company inevitably acquires or owns the shares of an affiliate and creates a circular shareholding to conclude a corporate merger or exercise a security right, it shall dispose of such shares within six months (Article 9).

A member company of a business group subject to limitations on cross-shareholding shall not have any shareholding in any affiliate that forms any circular shareholding. The foregoing also applies to additional shareholdings in an affiliate that has already formed a circular shareholding.[10] Similar to the case of cross-shareholding, if a company has acquired and created a circular shareholding in proportion to the shares involved in a corporate merger or stock transfer, the company shall dispose of the shares within a specified period. Unlike the rule on cross-shareholding, however, the provision governing circular shareholding does not require the elimination of the circular shareholding that had existed before the business group became subject to the regulation (Article 9(2)).

A member company of a business group subject to limitations on cross-shareholding that is engaged in financial business or insurance business shall not exercise its voting rights with respect to the shares acquired or held by it in its domestic affiliates.[11] It can still vote at the general meeting of shareholders of a listed affiliate, limited to the election and/or dismissal of directors, the amendment of the articles of incorporation, a corporate merger, and the transfer of business. For this purpose, the member company and a related party's combined number of shares eligible for voting shall not exceed 15%. If a member company acquires or holds the shares to engage in the finance or insurance business, it can exercise voting rights even at an affiliate (Article 11).

The Monopoly Regulation and Fair Trade Act—Restrictions on behavior of the holding company

In 1986, the government prohibited the holding company system out of the concern that corporates might take advantage of the governance structure to concentrate economic power. In more than ten years, it was reinstated in 1999 for the enhancement of the ownership transparency and management efficiency such as through restructuring, along with a few measures to mitigate the risk of economic power concentration. It lacked, however, the incentives for a conglomerate to convert to a holding company when it already had a controlling power such as through circular shareholding, which led to ongoing deregulation of the holding company system.

According to the existing antitrust provisions, a holding company shall hold a minimum of 40% of the shares of a subsidiary. The threshold is lower at a minimum of 20% if the subsidiary is a listed firm. The same applies to a sub-subsidiary, while a sub-sub-subsidiary shall be entirely owned by a sub-subsidiary. A holding company shall not hold the shares of an affiliate that is not its subsidiary or sub-subsidiary. It shall neither hold any shares of a non-affiliate exceeding 5%. Meanwhile, the Fair Trade Act does not allow a holding company to own a financial institution and a non-financial institution at the same time, to separate financial and industrial capital (Article 8(2)). Of business conglomerates subject to regulations, three are financial holding companies, and 19 are non-financial ones.

Also commonly observed is a business conglomerate that is not a holding company and holds the shares of a financial company, which raised the need for comprehensive supervision of financial conglomerates. Notably, in advanced financial markets, including the EU, discussions are underway on how to supervise financial conglomerates. In the past, Korea witnessed risk contagion to a financial company affiliated with a business group.[12] Against this backdrop, the Financial Services Commission and the Financial Supervisory Service published in June 2018 the Guidelines of Best Practices for Supervision of Financial Conglomerates, which is now in the pilot implementation stage.

The Guidelines define that if a business group has two or more financial companies in it, the financial companies collectively form a financial conglomerate. The new supervisory rule applies to the financial companies whose combined aggregate assets amount to KRW 5 trillion or more. The company at the top rank of the financial conglomerate becomes a representative company, which must disclose the matters concerning the financial conglomerate's ownership/governance structure, group-level risk management system, capital adequacy, related party transactions, and risk concentration, among others. A financial conglomerate that is a member of a business group shall assess and control the contagion risk where the financial or management risk of the industrial companies is transferred to the financial firms due to the issues like credit exposure, related party transactions and corporate governance. A representative company is subject to an annual risk management assessment comprising 18 assessment items under four categories of the risk management system, capital adequacy, related party transaction/risk concentration and governance/conflict of interests. A bill currently pending at the National Assembly captures the points mentioned above.

The Corporate Law

The Corporate Law neither defines a business group nor cites the Monopoly Regulation and Fair Trade Act. Instead, the code applies to an individual company. The harmful effects of a large business group such as damage to minority shareholders occur as a consequence of the actions taken by a specific company. In this sense, not only the regulations against business groups but also those against individual companies may prove useful when it comes to rectifying the problems posed by a large business group. The following details specific company-level regulations outlined in the Corporate Law but relevant to corporate governance of a conglomerate:

The controlling shareholder of a business group exerts influence at all member companies even if he/she does not hold a director position at any of them. For this reason, the Corporate Law recognises that a person who is not a director is still liable for damages against the company and/or a third party if he/she exerted influence, and ordered the execution of business activity or executed the same himself/herself. Shareholders are also entitled to the right to file a derivative suit (Article 401(2)).

The Corporate Law stipulates under Article 397-2 that *no director shall use business opportunities of the company that are likely to be of present or future benefit to the company, on his/her own account or on the account of a third party, without the approval of the board of directors*[13]. It further requires a board approval when a director, his/her spouse, his/her lineal ascendant or descendant, or a company they own 50% or more of the shares wishes to conduct a transaction with the company. Both cases require two-thirds of affirmative votes from the board (Article 398).

Disclosure by business groups

As mentioned above, a member company of a conglomerate shall disclose the matters about the business group to which it belongs. The disclosure shall include individual member companies' respective ownership details, cross-shareholdings or transactions between affiliates. Nonetheless, it is not enough to wholly understand the business group as an entity and track any changes. To provide the missing group-level picture, the KFTC has disclosed the ownership landscape, the percentage of shares owned by corporate leaders and related parties, circular shareholding details and governance structure since 2012.

The antitrust watchdog revealed that the shares held by all the related parties[14] at the 52 conglomerates controlled by a natural person reached 57.9%, and the shares owned by the natural person and his/her family[15] was 4%. Over the last 20 years, the top ten business groups saw the shares owned by their related parties grow while the shares held by the natural person controlling shareholder continued dropping, widening the control-ownership disparity (See Figure 5.1 and Table 5.1).

Figure 5.1. Top ten business groups' 20 years change in internal ownership

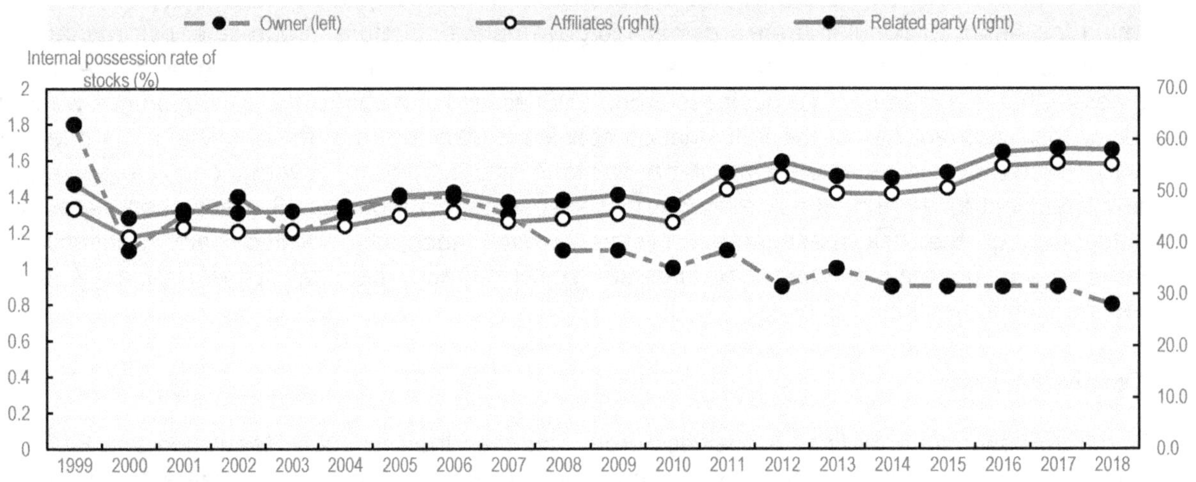

Source: Press release dated 27 August 2018 from Korea Fair Trade Commission.

Table 5.1. Top ten business groups' 20 years change in internal ownership

Division (%)	'99	'01	'03	'05	'07	'09	'11	'13	'15	'17	'18
Owner	1.8	1.3	1.2	1.4	1.3	1.1	1.1	1.0	0.9	0.9	**0.8**
Owner family including owner	-	3.1	3.5	3.6	3.4	3.3	2.9	3.0	2.7	2.5	**2.5**
Affiliates	46.6	43.0	42.4	45.3	44.1	45.6	50.3	49.6	50.6	55.5	**55.2**
Shares owned by related parties	51.5	46.4	46.2	49.2	47.9	49.3	53.5	52.9	53.6	58.3	**58.0**

Source: Press release dated 27 August 2018 from Korea Fair Trade Commission

The KFTC's report on corporate governance details the portion of the member companies whose controlling shareholder serves as a director, the operation of the board of directors and the tools to protect minority shareholders such as cumulative voting. According to the 2018 report, 21.8% of the member companies had the controlling shareholder or his/her family as a director. In a further breakdown, 46.7% of them were core businesses, 86.4% holding companies and 65.4% subject to the regulation on tunneling. As for the second or third generation of a controlling shareholder, 75.3% of the firms they served as director were subject to the rule on tunneling or out of the law's boundary.

The report continued that more conglomerates had in place a non-mandatory related-party committee and a compensation committee under the board, but it was questionable whether deliberation got underway faithfully. The KFTC's report further said that more than 99.5% of the proposals put to the vote at these board committees received support by the directors. 81.7% of the proposals to approve a private agreement with a related-party did not even mention the rationale. Lastly, listed member companies of a conglomerate did not reach the averages of the entire listed companies in terms of the adoption of cumulative voting, written voting and electronic voting.

The KFTC analyses ownership and governance structures that investors find it hard to understand intuitively and provides quality information for them. By doing so, the Commission contributes to increased market scrutiny and incentivises voluntary improvements on the part of large business groups.

Related-party dealings

Transactions between companies under the same business group can raise the competitiveness of the involved companies by acting as a substitute for an external market in the absence of an efficient outside market. At the same time, it may cause an undue wealth transfer from minority shareholders to the controlling shareholder. The Corporate Law has provisions on the use of corporate opportunities and requires board approval before a transaction if the directors and the company have conflicting interests. The rules are directed at preventing potential problems while acknowledging the merit of a related-party deal. The Monopoly Regulation and Fair Trade Act also has provisions that allow related-party dealings for efficiency, security and emergency purposes. The same code sets forth the conditions that constitute a related party transaction involving the taking of private benefits of control and prohibits such transactions. The following is a high-profile example where the involved companies were levied a fine after the provision banning tunneling became effective. The case is now with court over the legitimacy of the fine.

Enforcement of the regulation on extraction of private benefits of control

In 2016, the KFTC fined Company A engaging in the transportation business and its affiliates Company B and C around KRW 1.4 billion, saying that the transactions between the three companies provided unjust benefit for the controlling shareholder and his family. The Commission also brought charges against the CEO/president of Company C named D, who is a child of the concerned business group's controlling shareholder.

The children of Company A's controlling shareholder wholly owned Company B, which engages in in-flight duty-free sales. The regulator saw that Company A did not receive a sales commission from Company B without a proper agreement and thereby transferred undue profits to the controlling shareholder and his family. The children of the controlling shareholder had the most shares of Company C as well, whose revenues mainly came from the operation of a call center on behalf of Company A. Since a telecommunications service provider invested in and offered Company C system equipment and maintenance service for the call center operation at no cost, Company C did not incur any expenses for equipment or maintenance support. Nonetheless, Company A paid Company C for system usage and maintenance service. The KFTC believed that the act constituted a dealing that transferred undue benefits to the controlling shareholder and his family.

It was a representative action taken by the KFTC on the undue transfer of private benefits between affiliates since the regulation on the act was first adopted, and it drew much attention from the public. The three companies involved in the case challenged the KFTC's action and filed administrative litigation. The court made a decision favorable to the plaintiff, citing that the competition authority failed to prove the illegality of the dealing. The case is now pending with the Supreme Court.

The Inheritance Tax and Gift Tax Act

Not only the Corporate Law and the Fair Trade Act but also the Inheritance Tax and Gift Tax Act regulates the extraction of private benefits of control. In 2011, the inheritance and gift tax law added a new provision, recognising that the profit generated by an intragroup transaction constitutes a gift given to the controlling shareholder and his/her family when such transaction exceeded the percentage prescribed by law. Specifically, when the revenues originating from an intragroup transaction account for more than 30%[16] of the total revenue of the concerned company and the controlling shareholder and his/her family collectively own more than 3%[17] of the shares at the company, the after-tax operating profit multiplied by the respective excess percentages is recognised as a gift.

The tax law does not prohibit the undue private interest taking by the controlling shareholder outright. It instead taxes the benefit coming from an intragroup dealing as a disincentive. Meanwhile, an issue has arisen that intragroup transaction might drop below the legal threshold through a corporate merger, division, business transfer, and the like. Then, it is no longer subject to the regulation even if the problematic transaction continued.

A full amendment to the Monopoly Regulation and Fair Trade Act

On 16 March 2018, the KFTC set up a special committee to overhaul its antitrust law with view to effectively responding to rapid changes in the economy and tidying up the code that underwent piecemeal amendments on an ongoing basis for years. The special committee consisted of 23 specialists including 22 from the private sector, with three sub-committees covering competition law, conglomerate regulation, and procedural law, respectively.

The sub-committee covering conglomerate regulation, which has relevance to this report, proposed to reform i) the conglomerate designation rule; ii) the restriction on voting rights at financial and insurance companies and the regulation on public-service corporations; iii) the ban on circular shareholding; iv) the law on the extraction of private benefits of control; v) the disclosure about overseas affiliates to make it more stringent; and vi) the holding company system. Based on the special committee's proposals, the KFTC made an announcement of the upcoming legislation in August the same year. The bill currently awaits the approval of the National Assembly.

Conglomerate Designation Rule

The full amendment revised the threshold for the designation as a "business group subject to limitations on cross-shareholding" from KRW 10 trillion to 0.5% of the gross domestic product (GDP), so that the threshold may flexibly move in line with economic growth. The new rule applies from the year after the year when 0.5% of the GDP exceeds KRW 10 trillion.

The government expects that the change will ease difficulties on the part of companies that may be caused by the constancy and unexpected turn of the threshold and raise the predictability of the designation.

In the meantime, as for the business groups subject to disclosure, the existing threshold remains unchanged at KRW 5 trillion. Since the disclosure requirement was adopted for the sole purpose of curbing the extraction of private benefits of control, apart from the economic concentration concern, the need for tying it to the size of the economy is minimal.

Restrictions on financial/insurance companies' voting rights and public-service corporations

In principle, the full amendment prohibits a public-service corporation belonging to a "business group subject to limitations on cross-shareholding" from exercising voting rights on the shares it holds at an affiliate. Same as the financial and insurance companies forming a business group, a public-service corporation is allowed to exercise voting rights at a listed affiliate on the agenda of electing/dismissing directors and conducting a corporate merger, among others. Still, it cannot vote to exceed 15% of the shares held by it and its related party combined. For the soft-landing of the new rule, the authorities will give a grace period, and reduce the maximum limit of the voting rights in stages over three years (30% → 25% → 20% → 15%).

If a public service corporation which is a member of a "business group subject to disclosure" intends to trade shares and engages in a transaction with an affiliate over a particular level, which shall be determined by the relevant Presidential Decree, it is required to obtain board approval and disclose the details.

The special committee mandated to revise the antitrust code advised that the newly amended law lowers the maximum limit of the voting rights that financial and insurance companies can exercise to 5%, and removes corporate mergers and transfer of business from the agenda list they can vote. The final amendment proposal did not accept the 5% limit, but it eliminated a merger and business transfer between affiliates from the agenda list available for voting.

Ban on Circular Shareholding

The special committee agreed that there is a benefit in keeping the ban on circular shareholding against potential business group candidates, even though the shareholding type has mostly disappeared in Korea. It then concluded that restricting voting rights instead of forcing the disposal of a circular shareholding is more in line with the principle of minimised damage or proportionality principle.

The full amendment requires that the voting right restrictions apply even to the existing shareholdings of a newly designated "business group subject to restrictions on cross-shareholding." The requirement is intended to discourage a business group candidate from creating or building up circular shareholding before being designated as a business group.

Regulation on Extraction of Private Benefits of Control

The proposal to fully amend the Monopoly Regulation and Fair Trade Act requires that a company whose controlling shareholder owns 20% or more of its shares be subject to the regulation on the extraction of the private benefit of control, regardless of whether the company is listed or not. The rule also applies to an affiliated company more than 50% owned by a company subject to the concerned regulation. The special committee's proposal was accepted without any conflicting view.

Strengthened disclosure of overseas affiliates

The special committee proposed that the controlling shareholder of a business group disclose the shareholdings or circular shareholding that an overseas affiliate has at the domestic affiliated companies, either directly or indirectly. The disclosure shall also include the matters about a foreign affiliate 20% or more owned by the controlling shareholder and its subsidiaries. The full amendment did not accept the part requiring disclosure about subsidiaries.

The Holding Company System

The special committee advised raising the ownership ratio thresholds at subsidiaries and sub-subsidiaries. It also proposed that joint ownership of a sub-subsidiary be prohibited and disclosure of related-party transactions by holding companies be strengthened to prevent the transfer of profits for private interest other than dividends. The full amendment raised the ownership thresholds at subsidiaries and sub-subsidiaries by ten percentage points to 30% for listed firms and 50% for unlisted firms. The new rule applies to a holding company that is newly incorporated or converted. Although the amendment does not apply to an existing holding company and its subsidiaries and sub-subsidiaries, a current holding company acquiring a new subsidiary or sub-subsidiary is subject to the regulation. The rule does not apply to a venture holding company to promote investment in the sector. As for the strengthened disclosure requirement on a holding company's related-party transactions, the Enforcement Decree shall specify it.

Conclusion

The Korean government has made efforts from diverse angles towards the improvement of corporate governance of large business groups since the early 2010s when economic democratisation emerged as a hot topic. Notably, the Corporate Law adopted a rule on the taking of corporate opportunities, and the Monopoly Regulation and Fair Trade Act added a provision on the extraction of private benefits of control. It is also notable that a mandatory disclosure requirement was imposed on large business groups, and the scope of the disclosure was expanded to include their ownership structure, among others.

The various policy measures that the Korean government has adopted over the years or is currently pushing for legislation testify to the fact that the government is undoubtedly aware of the concerns local and global investors have about business conglomerates in the country. Although it is not radically fast-paced, the reform is progressing step by step in the right direction that is in line with the G20/OECD Principles of Corporate Governance.

The government is equally aware that forceful regulation is not a proper solution when it comes to corporate governance. Instead, it takes a prudent and market-friendly approach of raising market awareness and asking companies for their voluntary efforts. A good example is the KFTC's action to induce market scrutiny by mandating companies to disclose their ownership structure and the matters about corporate governance, their transactions involving a related party and the matters about a business group.

In addition to the regulatory measures to improve corporate governance that this report highlighted, the government has also tried to provide support for sharpening the competitiveness of the companies and invigorating their business activities in an ever-changing business environment. The Corporate Law reduced the liability to be borne by directors to incentivise creative and entrepreneurial decision-making. For increased flexibility in the large business group regulation, the law also raised the threshold for the designation of a business group subject to limitations on cross-shareholding. The government has worked hard to strike the right balance between keeping the merits of a business group system and minimising the side-effects. Going forward, it will continue this endeavor and spare no effort to create an environment where companies, investors, and all stakeholders communicate more and better.

References

OECD (2015), *G20/OECD Principles of Corporate Governance*, OECD Publishing, Paris, https://doi.org/10.1787/9789264236882-en.

FSC and FSS (2018), Plan for Comprehensive Supervision of Financial Conglomerates, 1 February, https://www.fsc.go.kr/downManager?bbsid=BBS0048&no=123601

KFTC (2019), The 2019 list of business groups subject to disclosure, 15 May.

Korea.net (2019), Korea sees the highest growth among OECD's 30-50 club members, http://www.korea.net/NewsFocus/Business/view?articleId=168953

Notes

[1] Korea sees the highest growth among OECD's 30-50 club members, 11 March 2019 Cheong wa dae

[2] Translation provided by the Korea Law Translation Center.

[3] For non-financial companies, a sum of total assets as of the end of the previous business year; for financial companies, an amount of the larger of the capital stock and total capital.

[4] Until 2016, the threshold for the business group restricted for cross-shareholding stood at KRW5 trillion. Following an amendment to the Fair Trade Act in 2017, the threshold rose, and the category of business groups subject to disclosure was newly installed.

[5] The 2019 list of business groups subject to disclosure, announced by the KFTC on 15 May 2019.

[6] Exclusive of the special purpose companies such as SPAC.

[7] 30% for listed firms and 20% for non-listed firms.

[8] Translation provided by the Korea Law Translation Center.

[9] Translation provided by the Korea Law Translation Center.

[10] Translation provided by the Korea Law Translation Center.

[11] Translation provided by the Korea Law Translation Center.

[12] Plan for Comprehensive Supervision of Financial Conglomerates, published by FSC and FSS, 1 February 2018

[13] Translation provided by the Korea Law Translation Center.

[14] Out of the total capital stock of an affiliate, the portion of the combined stock value held by the controlling shareholder and related parties including family members and affiliates.

[15] The percentage of the shares held by the controlling shareholder and his/her family.

[16] 50% for small companies and 40% for stable mid-sized companies. Up to the ratios, the law recognizes intra-group trading without having an issue of private-benefit taking.

[17] 10% for small and mid-sized companies. This includes indirect shareholding via an affiliate, and the law uses the term "marginal percentage of shareholding."

www.ingramcontent.com/pod-product-compliance
Lightning Source LLC
LaVergne TN
LVHW081414110826
845149LV00010B/1738

* 9 7 8 9 2 6 4 7 5 2 0 8 5 *